# SEPHER YETZIRAH: THE BOOK OF CREATION

Two Versions, Explaining Jewish Mystical Philoshophy and the Cabala

*Attributed to*
## Rabbi Akiba Ben Joseph

*Translations by*
## Rev. Dr. Isidor Kalisch and Knut Stenring

## THE BOOK TREE
San Diego, California

Originally published
1877
by L. H. Frank & Co.
New York
and
1923
William Rider & Son, Limited
London

ISBN 978-1-58509-282-6

Cover layout and design
by Toni Villalas

Published by
**The Book Tree**
**P.O. Box 16476**
**San Diego, CA 92176**
**www.thebooktree.com**

We provide fascinating and educational products to help awaken the public to new ideas and
information that would not be available otherwise.
Call 1 (800) 700-8733 for our *FREE BOOK TREE CATALOG*.

# ספר יצירה׃

# SEPHER YEZIRAH.

## A BOOK ON CREATION;

OR,

## THE JEWISH METAPHYSICS

OF

## REMOTE ANTIQUITY.

With English Translation, Preface, Explanatory Notes and Glossary,

BY

### Rev. Dr. ISIDOR KALISCH,

Author of the "Guide for Rational Inquiries into the Biblical Scriptures,"
"Tœne des Morgenlandes," Translator of "Nathan the Wise"
from the German, etc., etc., etc.

NEW YORK:

L. H. FRANK & CO., PUBLISHERS AND PRINTERS,
No. 32½ Bowery.

1877.

# PREFACE.

This metaphysical essay, called "Sepher Yezirah," (book on creation, or cosmogony,) which I have endeavored to render into English, with explanatory notes, is considered by all modern literati as the first philosophical book that ever was written in the Hebrew language. But the time of its composition and the name of its author have not yet been ascertained, despite of the most elaborate researches of renowned archaeologists. Some maintain that this essay is mentioned in the Talmud treatise Sanhedrin, p. 66 b. and ibid. 67 b. which passage is according to the commentary of Rashi, to treatise Erubin, p. 63 a., a reliable historical notice. Hence this book was known already in the second or at the beginning of the third century of the Christian Era. The historian, Dr. Graetz, tries to show very ingeniously in his work, entitled "Gnosticism," p. 104 and 110, that it was written in the early centuries of the Christian Church, especially when the ideas and views of the Gnostics were in vogue. This opinion, however, he afterwards revoked. (See Dr. Graetz's "History of the Jews," Vol. V, p. 315 in a note.)

Dr. Zunz, the Nestor of the Jewish Rabbis in Europe, maintains that we have to look for the genesis of the book "Yezirah" in the Geonic period, (700 —1000), and that it was consequently composed in a post-talmudical time. But if so, it is very strange that Saadjah Gaon, who lived in the tenth, and Judah Halevi, who lived in the twelfth century, represented the book "Yezirah" as a very ancient work. Therefore it seems to me, that Dr. Graetz had no sufficient cause to repudiate his assertion concerning the age of this book; because all the difficulties which he himself and others raised against his supposition, fall to the ground, when we consider that the most ancient works, holy as well as profane, had one and the same fate, namely, that from age to age more or less interpolations were made by copyists and commentators. Compare also Prof. Tenneman's "Grundriss der Geschichte der Philosophie," improved by Prof. Wendt, p. 207.

Tradition, which ascribes the authorship of this book to the patriarch Abraham, is fabulous, as can be proved by many reasons; but the idea that Rabbi Akiba, who lived about the beginning of the second century, composed the book "Yezirah," is very likely possible. Be this as it may, it is worth while to know the extravagant hypotheses which ancient Jewish philosophers and theologians framed as soon as they began to contemplate and to reason, endeavoring to combine oriental and Greek theories. Although there is an exuberance of weeds, we will find, nevertheless, many germs of truisms, which are of the greatest importance. A Christian theologian, Johann Friedrich von Meyer D. D., remarked very truly in his German preface to the book "Yezirah," published in Leipzig, 1830: "This book is for two reasons highly important: in the first place, that the real Cabala, or mystical doctrine of the Jews, which must be carefully distinguished from its excrescences, is in close connection and perfect accord with the Old and New Testaments; and in the second place, that the knowledge of it is of great importance to the philosophical inquirers, and can not be put aside. Like a cloud permeated by beams of light which makes one infer that there is more light behind it, so do the contents of this book, enveloped in obscurity, abound in coruscations of thought, reveal to the mind that there is a still more effulgent light lurking somewhere, and thus inviting us to a further contemplation and investigation, and at the same time demonstrating the danger of a superficial investigation, which is so prevalent in modern times, rejecting that which can not be understood at first sight."

I shall now try to give a sketch of the system as it is displayed in the book "Yezirah," which forms a link in the chain of the ancient theoretical speculations of philosophers, who were striving to ascertain the truth mainly by reasoning a-priori, and who imagined that it is thus possible to permeate all the secrets of nature. It teaches that a first cause, eternal, all-wise, almighty and holy, is the origin and the centre of the whole universe, from whom gradually all beings emanated. Thought, speech and action are an inseparable unity in the divine being; God made or created, is metaphorically expressed by the word: writing. The Hebrew language and its characters correspond mostly with the things they designate, and thus holy thoughts, Hebrew language and its reduction to writing, form a unity which produce a creative effect.*

The self-existing first cause called the creation into existence by quantity and quality; the former represented by ten numbers, (Sephiroth,) the latter by twenty-two letters, which form together thirty-two ways of the divine wisdom. Three of the twenty-two letters, namely, Aleph, Mem, Sheen, are the mothers, or the first elements, from which came forth the primitive matter of the world: air, water and fire, that have their parallel in man, (male and female): breast, body and head, and in the year: moisture, cold and heat. The other seven double and twelve‡ simple letters are then represented as stamina, from which other spheres or media of existence emanated.

Man is a microcosm, as the neck separates rationality from vitality, so does diaphragm the vitality from the vegetativeness.

---

*Thus for instance, they imagined that the name of Jehovah, יהוה is by reversing the alphabet; מצפץ (mzpz); mem signifies the letter jod, zaddi, the letter he, and pe, the letter wav. These unmeaning sounds, they said, have magic power. Some maintained that the Hebrew language consists of twenty-two consonants, because being the complex of all beings, its number is equal to the most perfect figure, namely, of the periphery, as it is well known that the diameter is always to the periphery as seven to twenty-two.

‡It was frequently observed by Jewish and Christian theologians, that the Marcosianic Gnostic system, as well as that of the Clementinians of the second century, contain many analogies and parallels with the book "Yezirah." Marcus divides the Greek alphabet into three parts, namely: nine mute consonants ἄφωνα, eight half vowels ἡμίφωνα, and seven vowels φωνήεντα, in order to give a clear idea of the peculiar constitution of his "Aeons." (Irenaeus Haer, I, 16.)

God stands in close connection with the Universe,
and just so is Tali connected with the world, that is,
an invisible, celestial or universal axis carries the
whole fabric. In the year by the sphere, in man by
the heart, and thus is the ruling spirit of God every-
where. Notwithstanding the decay of the individual,
the genus is produced by the antithesis of man and
wife.

Hebrew commentaries on the book "Yezirah" were
composed by: first, Saadjah Gaon, of Fajum in
Egypt, (892—942); second, Rabbi Abraham ben
Dior Halevi; third, Rabbi Moses ben Nachman;
fourth, Elieser of Germisa; fifth, Moses Botarel; sixth,
Rabbi Eliah Wilna: The book "Yezirah," together
with all these commentaries, was published in 1860,
in the city of Lemberg. But although the commentator Saadjah was a sober minded scholar in a
superstitious age, a good Hebrew grammarian, a renowned theologian and a good translator of the Hebrew Pentateuch, Isaiah and Job into the Arabian
language, his ideas and views were, nevertheless,
very often much benighted. See his comments on
Yez. Chap. I, etc., etc.; his notes on "Yezirah" Chap.
III, 2, prove undoubtedly that he had no knowledge
whatever of natural science, and therefore his annotations on the book "Yezirah" are of little or no use
at all. All the other commentaries mentioned above,
together with all quotations of other expounders of
the same book, contain nothing but a medley of arbitrary, mystical explanations and sophistical distor-
tions of scriptural verses, astrological notions, orient-

al superstitions, a metaphysical jargon, a poor knowledge of physics and not a correct elucidation of the
ancient book; they drew mostly from their own imagination, and credited the author of "Yezirah" with
saying very strange things which he never thought
of. I must not omit to mention two other Hebrew
commentaries, one by Judah Halevi, and the other
by Ebn Ezra, who lived in the first part of the twelfth
century. They succeeded in explaining the book "Yezirah in a sound scientific manner, but failed in
making themselves generally understood, on account
of the superstitious age in which they lived, and the
tenacity with which the people in that period adhered
to the marvelous and supernatural; they found, therefore, but few followers, and the book "Yezirah" remained to the public an enigma and an ancient curios-
ity, giving rise to a system of metaphysical delirium,
called Cabala.

Translations of the book "Yezirah" and comments
thereon by learned Christian authors are: first, a
translation of the book "Yezirah" with explanatory
notes in the Latin language, by Wilhelm Postellus,
Paris, France, 1552; second, another Latin version is
contained in Jo. Pistorii artis cabalistical scriptorum,
Tom I, p. 869, sqq., differing from that of Postellus.
Some are of the opinion that John Reuchlin, while
others maintain that Paul Riccius was the author of
it. (See Wolfii Biblioth. Hebr. Tom., I, Chap. 1.)
Third, Rittangel published the book "Yezirah," 1642,
at Amsterdam, entitled: "Liber Yezirah qui Abra-
hamo patriarchae adscribitur, una cum commentario

Rabbi Abraham F. D. (filii Dior) super 32 Semitis Sapientiae, a quibus liber Yezirah incipit. Translatus et notis illustratus, a Joanne Stephano Rittangelio, ling. Orient. in Elect. Acad. Regiomontana Prof. extraord. Amstelodami ap. Jo. and Jodoc. Janssonios," 1642, in quarto; fourth, Johann Friedrich von Mayer, D. D., published the book "Yezirah" in Hebrew with a translation and explanatory notes in the German language, Leipzig, 1830.

All these translations are out of print and are rarely found even in well regulated libraries. I was so fortunate as to obtain a copy of Dr. Mayer's edition of the book "Yezirah." He states in the preface to it, that he had a copy of Postellus' translation in manuscript as well as some others, and compared them. The explanatory notes given by this author are, nevertheless, insufficient and sometimes very incorrect. The present translation is, as far as I could ascertain, the first that was ever published in the English language. Again, I have to add that I have not only endeavored to correct a great many mistakes and erroneous ideas of my predecessors, but I have also endeavored to give more complete annotations. I therefore hope that the candid reader will consider the great difficulties I had to overcome in this still unbeaten way of the ancient Jewish spiritual region, and will receive with indulgence this new contribution to archaeological knowledge.

Dr. ISIDOR KALISCH.

# PUBLISHER'S INTRODUCTION

This book is considered to be the oldest known Jewish mystical text and is now an important part of Cabalistic studies. It first appeared in historical records during the first century C.E., but its principles had been passed down for centuries before this, with Jewish scholars believing that the patriarch Abraham had received the teachings directly. It is written from the perspective of an observer who is relating the work of God's creation step by step, as it unfolds. It covers not only the creation of the universe, but the formation of the earth and humanity as well. It reveals how the 22 letters of the Hebrew alphabet work symbolically and interact with one another, through God, to bring about our physical world. Most cultures agree that God created the universe, our world and our bodies but many creation stories beyond this one are less complete. By looking deeply at this story and studying its message, one can come away with meaningful insights that will not be available elsewhere. This book is often considered to be a meditative text, focused upon more in the first translation by Kalisch, and also as a magical text, covered more clearly in the second version by Stenring. If something is not made clear in one version it can be likely be found in the other, which is what makes this book so interesting. It is a very powerful mystical work and having access to two separate translations in one volume is of immense importance.

Paul Tice
The Book Tree

# FOREWORD

The service Dr. Kalisch rendered in 1877 by his first English translation of the Sepher Yezirah has grown even greater with the passing years. Other translations, it is true, have a certain merit; none the less, none has surpassed and few have equalled the work which he did.

This is so not because Dr. Kalisch was Jewish and other translators were not; but rather because his translation was prompted by motives unmixed with mistaken notions of the author's intent. He dealt with it reverently as the earliest example of Hebrew metaphysical writing and not as a brief for a particular school of magical legerdemain in the realm of thought.

One readily forgives him, then, for calling the Cabala a system of metaphysical delirium, for such it became in the hands of those whose mental discipline was small and whose imagination large. He rescued the Sepher Yezirah from the unworthy use to which such writers were subjecting it.

Without question, the Sepher Yezirah is a fundamental source of Cabalistic thought, but it should be remembered, as Dr. Johann Friedrich von Meyer pointed out in his preface to the German translation of 1830, a distinction must always be made between the real Cabala and the excrescences which have developed around it. Unfortunately, for most, those excrescences are the Cabala.

Dr. Kalisch's real service lay in restoring the work as a sound metaphysical treatise worthy of the attention of all seriously interested in the development of such concepts.

Originally, the Cabala was conducive to such concepts, and had Cabalists confined themselves solely to the

Yezirah's pattern and not ventured beyond it in extensions of thought based on fundamental misconceptions, the extravagances of eighteenth and nineteenth century mysticism would have been avoided and the Cabala would today be seen as a steady and reliable beacon in a world of dark and confused thinking. But for that result, the human mind itself would have had to be differently constituted.

Modern systems of thought—ethical, religious, metaphysical—have nevertheless been permeated with ideas directly traceable to the Cabala. Esoteric societies and fraternal organizations have drawn largely from it for their ritualistic teaching and procedure—oftentimes being altogether unaware of their indebtedness.

The Ancient and Mystical Order Rosae Crucis has numbered among its members in the past many who were known to be Cabalists, and today its membership is kept informed of the essential characteristics. It is in the attempt to make available authentic information on the subject that this reprinting of Dr. Kalisch's translation of the Sepher Yezirah is undertaken. There is little doubt that the careful and properly discriminating reader will be adequately rewarded for the time he spends in the study of this invaluable little essay.

Rosicrucian Park     JOEL DISHER
October 13, 1948     Literary Research Dept.
                    The Rosicrucian Order. AMORC

# SEPHER YEZIRAH.

## CHAPTER I.

### SECTION 1.

Yah,[1] the Lord of hosts, the living God, King of
the Universe, Omnipotent, All-Kind and Merciful,
Supreme and Extolled, who is Eternal, Sublime
and Most-Holy, ordained (formed) and created the
Universe in thirty-two[2] mysterious paths[3] of wisdom
by three[4] Sepharim, namely: 1) S'for סְפָר; 2) Sip-
pur סִפּוּר; and 3) Sapher סֵפֶר which are in Him one and
the same. They consist of a decade out of nothing[5]
and of twenty-two fundamental letters. He divided
the twenty-two consonants into three divisions: 1)
three אִמּוֹת mothers, fundamental letters or first elements; 2) seven double; and 3) twelve simple consonants.

### SECTION 2.

The decade[6] out of nothing is analogous to that of
the ten fingers (and toes) of the human body, five
parallel to five, and in the centre of which is the
covenant with the only One, by the word of the
tongue and the rite of Abraham.

### SECTION 3.

Ten are the numbers out of nothing, and not the
number nine, ten and not eleven. Comprehend this
great wisdom, understand this[7] knowledge, inquire
into it and ponder on it, render it evident and lead[8]
the Creator back to His throne again.

---

1) See Notes commencing on Page 50

# ס פ ר יצירה·

---

## פרק ראשון·

### מ ש נ ה א·

בִּשְׁלֹשִׁים וּשְׁתַּיִם נְתִיבוֹת פְּלִיאוֹת חָכְמָה חָקַק
יָהּ יְהֹוָה צְבָאוֹת אֱלֹהִים חַיִּים וּמֶלֶךְ עוֹלָם אֵל שַׁדַּי
רַחוּם וְחַנּוּן רָם וְנִשָּׂא שׁוֹכֵן עַד מָרוֹם וְקָדוֹשׁ שְׁמוֹ
וּבָרָא אֶת עוֹלָמוֹ בִשְׁלֹשָׁה סְפָרִים *בִּסְפָר וְסִפּוּר
וְסֵפֶר: עֶשֶׂר סְפִירוֹת בְּלִימָה וְעֶשְׂרִים וּשְׁתַּיִם
אוֹתִיּוֹת יְסוֹד: שָׁלֹשׁ אִמּוֹת וְשֶׁבַע כְּפוּלוֹת וּשְׁתֵּים
עֶשְׂרֵה פְּשׁוּטוֹת:

### מ ש נ ה ב·

עֶשֶׂר סְפִירוֹת בְּלִימָה כְּמִסְפַּר עֶשֶׂר אֶצְבָּעוֹת
חָמֵשׁ כְּנֶגֶד חָמֵשׁ וּבְרִית יָחִיד מְכֻוֶּנֶת בְּאֶמְצַע
בְּמִלַּת הַלָּשׁוֹן וּבְמִלַּת הַמָּעוֹר:

### מ ש נ ה ג·

עֶשֶׂר סְפִירוֹת בְּלִימָה עֶשֶׂר וְלֹא תֵשַׁע עֶשֶׂר וְלֹא
אַחַת עֶשְׂרֵה הָבֵן בְּחָכְמָה וַחֲכַם בְּבִינָה בָּחוֹן בָּהֶם
וַחֲקוֹר מֵהֶם וְהַעֲמֵד דָּבָר עַל בּוּרְיוֹ וְהוֹשֵׁב יוֹצֵר
עַל־מְכוֹנוֹ:

---

*נ"א. בְּסֵפֶר וְסוֹפֵר וְסִפּוּר:

## SECTION 4.

The decade out of nothing has the following ten infinitudes:

| | | | | |
|---|---|---|---|---|
| 1) | The beginning[9] infinite. | 6) | The depth infinite. | |
| 2) | " end " | 7) | " East " | |
| 3) | " good " | 8) | " West " | |
| 4) | " evil[10] " | 9) | " North " | |
| 5) | " height " | 10) | " South " | |

and the only Lord God, the faithful King, rules over all from His holy habitation for ever and ever.

## SECTION 5.

The appearance of the ten spheres out of nothing is like a flash of lightning, being without an end, His word is in them, when they go and return; they run by His order like a whirlwind and humble themselves before His throne.

## SECTION 6.

The decade of existence out of nothing has its end linked to its beginning and its beginning linked to its end, just as the flame is wedded to the live coal; because the Lord is one and there is not a second one, and before one what wilt thou count?[11]

## SECTION 7.

Concerning the number ten of the spheres of existence out of nothing keep thy tongue from speaking and thy mind from pondering on it, and if thy mouth urges thee to speak, and thy heart to think about it, return! as it reads: "And the living creatures ran and returned," (Ezekiel 1, 14.) and upon this[12] was the covenant made.

## משנה ד.

עֶשֶׂר סְפִירוֹת בְּלִימָה מִדָּתָן עֶשֶׂר שֶׁאֵין לָהֶם
סוֹף עוֹמֶק רֵאשִׁית וְעוֹמֶק אַחֲרִית עוֹמֶק טוֹב וְעוֹמֶק
רָע עוֹמֶק רוֹם וְעוֹמֶק תַּחַת עוֹמֶק מִזְרָח וְעוֹמֶק
מַעֲרָב עוֹמֶק צָפוֹן וְעוֹמֶק דָּרוֹם אָדוֹן יָחִיד אֵל מֶלֶךְ
נֶאֱמָן מוֹשֵׁל בְּכֻלָּם מִמְּעוֹן קָדְשׁוֹ עַד עֲדֵי עַד:

## משנה ה.

עֶשֶׂר סְפִירוֹת בְּלִימָה צְפִיָּתָן כְּמַרְאֵה הַבָּזָק
וְתַכְלִיתָן אֵין לָהֶן קֵץ דְּבָרוֹ כָהֵן בְּרָצוֹא וָשׁוֹב
וּלְמַאֲמָרוֹ כְּסוּפָה יִרְדֹּפוּ וְלִפְנֵי כִסְאוֹ הֵם מִשְׁתַּחֲוִים:

## משנה ו.

עֶשֶׂר סְפִירוֹת בְּלִימָה נָעוּץ סוֹפָן בַּתְחִלָּתָן וּתְחִלָּתָן
בְּסוֹפָן כְּשַׁלְהֶבֶת קְשׁוּרָה* בְּנַחֶלֶת שֶׁאָדוֹן יָחִיד וְאֵין
לוֹ שֵׁנִי וְלִפְנֵי אֶחָד מַה אַתָּה סוֹפֵר:

## משנה ז.

עֶשֶׂר סְפִירוֹת בְּלִימָה בְּלוֹם פִּיךָ מִלְּדַבֵּר וְלִבְּךָ
מִלְּהַרְהֵר וְאִם רָץ פִּיךָ לְדַבֵּר וְלִבְּךָ לְהַרְהֵר שׁוּב
לְמָקוֹם שֶׁלְּכָךְ נֶאֱמַר וְהַחַיּוֹת רָצוֹא וָשׁוֹב וְעַל דָּבָר
זֶה נִכְרַת בְּרִית:

---

*) רַבֵּינוּ הַאָיי גָּאוֹן ז״ל כָּתַב בְּסֵפֶר הַקְּמֵיצָה וַז״ל כָּתַב בַּעַל סֵפֶר יְצִירָה
כְּשַׁלְהֶבֶת שׂוֹרָה בְּנַחֲלֶת:

## SECTION 8.

The following are the ten categories of existence out of nothing:

1) The spirit of the living God, praised and glorified be the name of Him who lives to all eternity. The articulate word of creative power, the spirit and the word are what we call the holy spirit.[13]

2) Air emanated from the spirit by which He formed and established twenty-two consonants, stamina. Three of them, however, are fundamental letters, or mothers, seven double and twelve simple consonants; hence the spirit is the first one.

3) Primitive water emanated from the air. He formed and established by it Bohu[14] (water, stones) mud and loam, made them like a bed, put them up like a wall, and surrounded them as with a rampart, put coldness upon them and they became dust, as it reads: "He says to the snow (coldness) be thou earth." (Job 37, 6.)

4) Fire or ether emanated from the water. He established by it the throne of glory, the Seraphim and Ophanim, the holy living creatures and the angels, and of these three He formed His habitation, as it reads: "Who made His angels spirits, His ministers a flaming fire." (Psalm 104, 4.) He selected three consonants from the simple ones which are in the hidden secret of three mothers or first elements: א"מ"ש, air, water and ether or fire. He sealed them with spirit and fastened them to His great name and sealed with it six dimensions.[15]

## מִשְׁנָה ח.

עֶשֶׂר סְפִירוֹת בְּלִימָה אַחַת רוּחַ אֱלֹהִים חַיִּים
בָּרוּךְ וּמְבוֹרָךְ שְׁמוֹ שֶׁל חַי הָעוֹלָמִים קוֹל וְרוּחַ
וְדִבּוּר וְהוּא רוּחַ הַקּוֹדֶשׁ: שְׁתַּיִם רוּחַ מֵרוּחַ חָקַק
וְחָצַב בָּהּ עֶשְׂרִים וּשְׁתַּיִם אוֹתִיּוֹת יְסוֹד שָׁלֹשׁ אִמּוֹת
וְשֶׁבַע כְּפוּלוֹת וּשְׁתֵּים עֶשְׂרֵה פְשׁוּטוֹת וְרוּחַ אַחַת
מֵהֶן: שָׁלֹשׁ מַיִם מֵרוּחַ חָקַק וְחָצַב בָּהֶן (עֶשְׂרִים
וּשְׁתַּיִם אוֹתִיּוֹת) תֹּהוּ וָבֹהוּ רֶפֶשׁ וָטִיט חֲקָקָן כְּמִין
עֲרוּגָה הִצִּיבָן* כְּמִין חוֹמָה סִכְּכָם‡ כְּמִין מַעֲזִיבָה
(וְיָצַק עֲלֵיהֶם שֶׁלֶג וְנַעֲשָׂה עָפָר שֶׁנֶּאֱמַר כִּי לַשֶּׁלֶג
יֹאמַר הֱוֵא אָרֶץ): אַרְבַּע אֵשׁ מִמַּיִם חָקַק וְחָצַב בָּהּ
כִּסֵּא הַכָּבוֹד שְׂרָפִים וְאוֹפַנִּים וְחַיּוֹת הַקּוֹדֶשׁ וּמַלְאֲכֵי
הַשָּׁרֵת וּמִשְּׁלָשְׁתָּן יָסַד מְעוֹנוֹ שֶׁנֶּאֱמַר עוֹשֶׂה
מַלְאָכָיו רוּחוֹת מְשָׁרְתָיו אֵשׁ לוֹהֵט בֵּירֵר שְׁלֹשָׁה
אוֹתִיּוֹת מִן הַפְּשׁוּטוֹת בְּסוֹד שָׁלֹשׁ אִמּוֹת אֶ״מֶ״שׁ‖
וּקְבָעָם בִּשְׁמוֹ הַגָּדוֹל וְחָתַם בָּהֶם שֵׁשׁ קְצָווֹת:

---

*) נוּסְחָא אַחֲרִינָא: חֲצָבָן:

‡) נ״א סִיכְּבָן:

‖) יֵשׁ הוֹסִיפוּ: חָתַם רוּחַ בְּעַד שָׁלֹשׁ:

5) He sealed[16] the height and turned towards above, and sealed it with          יהו

6) He sealed the depth, turned towards below and sealed it with          היו

7) He sealed the east and turned forward, and sealed it with          ויה

8) He sealed the west and turned backward, and sealed it with          והי

9) He sealed the south and turned to the right and sealed it with          יוה

10) He sealed the north and turned to the left and sealed it with          הוי

### SECTION 9.

These are the ten spheres of existence out of nothing. From the spirit of the living God emanated air, from the air, water, from the water, fire or ether, from the ether, the height and the depth, the East and West, the North and South.

--------

# CHAPTER II.

### SECTION 1.

There are twenty-two letters, stamina. Three of them, however, are the first elements, fundamentals or mothers, seven double and twelve simple consonants. The three fundamental letters א"מ"ש have as their basis the balance. In one scale[17] is the merit and in the other criminality, which are placed in equilibrium by the tongue. The three fundamental letters א"מ"ש signify, as מ is mute like the water and ש hissing like the fire, there is א among them, a breath of air which reconciles them.

### SECTION 2.

The twenty-two letters which form the stamina

חָמֵשׁ חָתַם רוּם וּפָנָה לְמַעֲלָה וַחֲתָמוּ  **בידהו**

שֵׁשׁ חָתַם תַּחַת וּפָנָה לְמַטָּה וַחֲתָמוּ  **בהיו**

שֶׁבַע חָתַם מִזְרָח וּפָנָה לְפָנָיו וַחֲתָמוּ  **בויה**

שְׁמוֹנָה חָתַם מַעֲרָב וּפָנָה לְאַחֲרָיו וַחֲתָמוּ  **בוהי**

תֵּשַׁע חָתַם דָּרוֹם וּפָנָה לִימִינוֹ וַחֲתָמוּ  **ביוה**

עֶשֶׂר חָתַם צָפוֹן וּפָנָה לִשְׂמֹאלוֹ וַחֲתָמוּ  **בהוי**

### מ ש נ ה   ט.

אֵלּוּ עֶשֶׂר סְפִירוֹת בְּלִימָה אַחַת רוּחַ אֱלֹהִים חַיִּים רוּחַ מֵרוּחַ מַיִם מֵרוּחַ אֵשׁ מִמַּיִם רוּם וְתַחַת מִזְרָח וּמַעֲרָב צָפוֹן וְדָרוֹם:

## פרק שני·

### מ ש נ ה   א.

עֶשְׂרִים וּשְׁתַּיִם אוֹתִיּוֹת יְסוֹד שָׁלֹשׁ אִמּוֹת וְשֶׁבַע כְּפוּלוֹת וּשְׁתֵּים עֶשְׂרֵה פְשׁוּטוֹת שָׁלֹשׁ אִמּוֹת אֶא״מ״שׁ יְסוֹדָן כַּף זְכוּת וְכַף חוֹבָה וְלָשׁוֹן חָק מַכְרִיעַ בִּנְתַּיִם שָׁלֹשׁ אִמּוֹת אֶא״מ״שׁ מ׳ דּוֹמֶמֶת שׁ׳ שׁוֹרֶקֶת א׳ אֲוֵיר רוּחַ מַכְרִיעַ בִּנְתַּיִם:

### מ ש נ ה   ב.

עֶשְׂרִים וּשְׁתַּיִם אוֹתִיּוֹת יְסוֹד חָקְקָן חָצְבָן חֲצָבָן צָרְפָן

after having been appointed and established by God, He combined, weighed and changed them, and formed by them all beings which are in existence, and all those which will be formed in all time to come.

## SECTION 3.

He established twenty-two letters, stamina, by the voice, formed by the breath of air and fixed them on five places in the human mouth, namely: 1) gutturals, א ה ח ע 2) palatals, ג י כ ק 3) linguals, ד ט ל נ ת 4) dentals, ז ש ס ר ץ 5) labials, ב ו מ ף

## SECTION 4.

He fixed the twenty-two letters, stamina, on the sphere like a wall with two hundred and thirty-one gates,[18] and turned the spheres forward and backward. For an illustration may serve the three letters, ע נ ג There is nothing better than joy, and nothing worse than sorrow or plague.[19]

## SECTION 5.

But how was it done? He combined,[20] weighed and changed: the א with all the other letters in succession, and all the others again with א; ב with all, and all again with ב; and so the whole series of letters.[21] Hence it follows that there are two hundred and thirty-one[22] formations, and that every creature and every word emanated from one name.[23]

## SECTION 6.

He created a reality out of nothing, called the nonentity into existence and hewed, as it were, colossal pillars from intangible air. This has been shown by the example of combining the letter א with

שָׁקְלָן וְהֵמִירָן וְצָר בָּהֶם אֶת כָּל הַיְצוּר וְאֶת כָּל
הֶעָתִיד לָצוּר:

## מ ש נ ה  ג.

עֶשְׂרִים וּשְׁתַּיִם אוֹתִיּוֹת יְסוֹד חָקְקָן בְּקוֹל חָצְבָן
בְּרוּחַ קָבְעָן בְּפֶה בְּחָמֵשׁ מְקוֹמוֹת אוֹתִיּוֹת אַהֲחַ"ע
בַּגָּרוֹן גִיכַ"ק בְּחֵיךְ דַטְלְנַ"ת בִּלָּשׁוֹן זַשְׂסְרָ"ץ בְּשִׁנַּיִם
בּוּמָ"ף בִּשְׂפָתַיִם:

## מ ש נ ה  ד.

עֶשְׂרִים וּשְׁתַּיִם אוֹתִיּוֹת יְסוֹד קָבְעָן בְּגַלְגַּל כְּמִין
חוֹמָה בְּרל"א שְׁעָרִים וְחוֹזֵר הַגַּלְגַּלִים פָּנִים וְאָחוֹר
וְסִימָן לַדָּבָר אֵין בְּטוֹבָה לְמַעֲלָה מֵעֹנֶג וְאֵין בְּרָעָה
לְמַטָּה מִנֶּגַע:

## מ ש נ ה  ה.

כֵּיצַד צְרָפָן שָׁקְלָן וְהֵמִירָן א עִם בָּ"לָן וְכָלָן עִם א
ב עִם בָּ"לָן וְכָלָן עִם ב וְחוֹזְרוֹת חָלִילָה וְנִמְצָאוֹת
בְּרל"א שְׁעָרִים וְנִמְצָא כָּל הַיְצוּר וְכָל הַדִּבּוּר יוֹצֵא
מִשֵּׁם* אֶחָד:

## מ ש נ ה  ו.

יָצַר מַמָּשׁ מִתֹּהוּ וְעָשָׂה אֶת אֵינוֹ יֶשְׁנוֹ וְחָצַב
עֲמוּדִים גְּדוֹלִים מֵאַוִיר שֶׁאֵינוֹ נִתְפָּס וְזֶה סִימָן אוֹת

---

all the other letters, and all the other letters with Aleph (א). He[24] predetermined, and by speaking created every creature and every word by one name. For an illustration may serve the twenty-two elementary substances by the primitive substance of Aleph[25] (א).

---

# CHAPTER III.

## SECTION 1.

The three first elements, א״מ״ש are typified by a balance, in one scale the merit and in the other the criminality, which are placed in equilibrium by the tongue. These three mothers, א״מ״ש are a great, wonderful and unknown mystery, and are sealed by six[26] rings, or elementary circles, namely: air, water and fire emanated from them, which gave birth to progenitors, and these progenitors gave birth again to some offspring.

## SECTION 2.

God appointed and established the three mothers א״מ״ש, combined, weighed and changed them, and formed by them three mothers א״מ״ש in the world, in the year and in man, male and female.

## SECTION 3.

The three mothers א״מ״ש in the world are: air, water and fire. Heaven was created from fire or ether; the earth (comprising sea and land) from the elementary water; and the atmospheric air from the elementary air, or spirit, which establishes the balance among them.

א עִם כֻּלָּן וְכֻלָּן עִם א צוֹפֶה וּמֵימַר וְעָשָׂה אֶת כָּל
הַיְצוּר וְאֶת כָּל הַדִּבּוּר שֵׁם אֶחָד וְסִימָן לַדָּבָר
עֶשְׂרִים וּשְׁתַּיִם חֲפָצִים בְּגוּף א :

## פרק שלישי.

### מ ש נ ה א.

שָׁלֹשׁ אִמּוֹת אֶמֶ"שׁ יְסוֹדָן כַּף זְכוּת וְכַף חוֹבָה
וְלָשׁוֹן חָק מַכְרִיעַ בְּנְתַּיִם שָׁלֹשׁ אִמּוֹת אֶמֶ"שׁ סוֹד
גָּדוֹל מוּפְלָא וּמְכֻסֶּה וְחָתוּם בְּשֵׁשׁ טַבָּעוֹת וְיָצְאוּ
מֵהֶם אֲוִיר וּמַיִם וְאֵשׁ וּמֵהֶם נוֹלְדוּ אָבוֹת וּמֵאָבוֹת
תּוֹלְדוֹת :

### מ ש נ ה ב.

שָׁלֹשׁ אִמּוֹת אֶמֶ"שׁ חָקְקָן חָצְבָן צְרָפָן שְׁקָלָן
וְהֶמִירָן וְצָר בָּהֶם שָׁלֹשׁ אִמּוֹת אֶמֶ"שׁ בָּעוֹלָם וְשָׁלֹשׁ
אִמּוֹת אֶמֶ"שׁ בַּשָּׁנָה וְשָׁלֹשׁ אִמּוֹת אֶמֶ"שׁ בַּנֶּפֶשׁ
זָכָר וּנְקֵבָה :

### מ ש נ ה ג.

שָׁלֹשׁ אִמּוֹת אֶמֶ"שׁ בָּעוֹלָם אֲוִיר וּמַיִם וְאֵשׁ שָׁמַיִם
נִבְרְאוּ מֵאֵשׁ וְאֶרֶץ נִבְרֵאת מִמַּיִם וַאֲוִיר מְרוּחַ
מַכְרִיעַ בְּנְתַּיִם :

---

*) נ"א וּמֵהֶן יוֹצְאִים אֵשׁ וּמַיִם וּמִתְחַלְּקִים זָכָר וּנְקֵבָה שָׁלֹשׁ אִמּוֹת
אֶמֶ"שׁ יְסוֹדָן וּמֵהֶן נוֹלְדוּ אָבוֹת שֶׁמֵּהֶם נִבְרָא הַכֹּל :

## Section 4.

The three mothers א"מ"ש produce in the year[27]: heat, coldness[28] and moistness. Heat was created from fire, coldness from water, and moistness from air which equalizes them.

## Section 5.

The three mothers א"מ"ש produce in man, male and female, breast, body and head. The head was created from fire, the breast from water, and the body from air, which places them in equilibrium.

## Section 6.

FIRST DIVISION. God let the letter Aleph (א) predominate in primitive air, crowned[29] it, combined one with the other,[30] and formed by them the air in the world, moistness in the year, and the breast in man, male and female; in male by א"מ"ש and in female by: א"ש"ם

## Section 7.

SECOND DIVISION. He let the letter Mem (מ) predominate in primitive water, and crowned it, combined one with the other, and formed by them the earth, (including land and sea) coldness in the year, and the belly in male and female; in male by א"מ"ש.[31] in female by: מ"ש"א

## Section 8.

THIRD DIVISION. He let the letter Sheen (ש) predominate in primitive fire, crowned it, combined one with the other, and formed by them, heaven in the world, heat in the year, and the head of male and female.[32]

## מ שנ ה ד.

שָׁלֹש אִמּוֹת אֶ״מֶ״שׁ בַּשָּׁנָה חוֹם וְקוֹר וּרְוָיָה חוֹם
נִבְרָא מֵאֵשׁ קוֹר נִבְרָא מִמַּיִם וּרְוָיָה מֵרוּחַ מַכְרִיעַ
בְּנְתַּיִם:

## מ שנ ה ה.

שָׁלֹש אִמּוֹת אֶ״מֶ״שׁ בְּנֶפֶשׁ זָכָר וּנְקֵבָה רֹאשׁ וּבֶטֶן
וּגְוִיָּה רֹאשׁ נִבְרָא מֵאֵשׁ וּבֶטֶן נִבְרָא מִמַּיִם וּגְוִיָּה
מֵרוּחַ מַכְרִיעַ בְּנְתַּיִם:

## מ שנ ה ו.

בָּבָא א. הִמְלִיךְ אוֹת א׳ בְּרוּחַ וְקָשַׁר לוֹ כֶּתֶר
וְצָרְפָן זֶה בָזֶה וְצָר בָּהֶם אַוִּיר בָּעוֹלָם רְוָיָה בְּשָׁנָה
גְוִיָּה בְּנֶפֶשׁ זָכָר בְּאֶ״מֶ״שׁ וּנְקֵבָה בְּאָ״שָׁ״ם:

## מ שנ ה ז.

בָּבָא ב. הִמְלִיךְ אוֹת מ׳ בְּמַיִם וְקָשַׁר לוֹ כֶּתֶר
וְצָרְפָן זֶה בָזֶה וְצָר בָּהֶם אֶרֶץ בָּעוֹלָם וְקוֹר בַּשָּׁנָה
וּבֶטֶן בְּנֶפֶשׁ זָכָר בְּאֶ״מֶ״שׁ* וּנְקֵבָה בְּמַ״שָׁ״א:

## מ שנ ה ח.

בָּבָא ג. הִמְלִיךְ אוֹת שׁ׳ בְּאֵשׁ וְקָשַׁר לוֹ כֶּתֶר
וְצָרְפָן זֶה בָזֶה וְצָר בָּהֶם שָׁמַיִם בָּעוֹלָם וְחוֹם בְּשָׁנָה
וְרֹאשׁ בְּנֶפֶשׁ זָכָר וּנְקֵבָה:

*) נ״א בְּמֶ״אֶ״שׁ:

# CHAPTER IV.

## SECTION 1.

The[33] seven double letters, בגד כפרת with a duplicity of pronunciation, aspirated and unaspirated, namely: בב, גג, דד, כב, פפ, רר, תת, serve as a model of softness and hardness, strength and weakness.

## SECTION 2.

Seven[34] double letters, בגד כפרת, shall, as it were, symbolize wisdom, wealth, fruitfulness, life, dominion, peace and beauty.

## SECTION 3.

Seven double letters serve to signify the antithesis to which human life is exposed. The antithesis of wisdom is foolishness; of wealth, poverty; of fruitfulness, childlessness; of life, death; of dominion, dependence; of peace, war; and of beauty, ugliness.

## SECTION 4.

The seven double consonants are analogous to the six dimensions: height and depth, East and West, North and South, and the holy temple that stands in the centre, which carries them all.

## SECTION 5.

The double consonants are seven, בגד כפרת and not six, they are seven and not eight; reflect upon this

# פרק רביעי·

### מ ש נ ה   א.

שֶׁבַע כְּפוּלוֹת בְּגַ״ד כַּפְרַ״ת מִתְנַהֲגוֹת בִּשְׁתֵּי
לְשׁוֹנוֹת בֵּי״ב גֵּי״ג דֵּי״ד כֵּי״כ פֵּי״פ רֵי״ר תֵּי״ת תַּבְנִית
רַךְ וְקָשֶׁה גִּבּוֹר וְחָלָשׁ:

### מ ש נ ה   ב.

שֶׁבַע כְּפוּלוֹת בְּגַ״ד כַּפְרַ״ת יְסוֹדָן חָכְמָה וְעוֹשֶׁר
וְזֶרַע וְחַיִּים וּמֶמְשָׁלָה שָׁלוֹם וְחֵן:

### מ ש נ ה   ג.

שֶׁבַע כְּפוּלוֹת בְּגַ״ד כַּפְרַ״ת בְּדִבּוּר וּבִתְמוּרָה
תְּמוּרַת חָכְמָה אִוֶּלֶת תְּמוּרַת עֹשֶׁר עוֹנִי תְּמוּרַת
זֶרַע שְׁמָמָה תְּמוּרַת הַחַיִּים מָוֶת תְּמוּרַת מֶמְשָׁלָה
עַבְדוּת תְּמוּרַת שָׁלוֹם מִלְחָמָה תְּמוּרַת חֵן כִּיעוּר:

### מ ש נ ה   ד.

שֶׁבַע כְּפוּלוֹת בְּגַ״ד כַּפְרַ״ת מַעֲלָה וּמַטָּה מִזְרָח
וּמַעֲרָב צָפוֹן וְדָרוֹם וְהֵיכַל הַקֹּדֶשׁ מְכָן בָּאֶמְצַע
וְהוּא נוֹשֵׂא אֶת כֻּלָּן:

### מ ש נ ה   ה.

שֶׁבַע כְּפוּלוֹת בְּגַ״ד כַּפְרַ״ת שִׁבְעָה וְלֹא שִׁשָּׁה

fact, inquire about it, and make it so evident, that[35] the Creator be acknowledged to be on His throne again.

### SECTION 6.

The seven double consonants, stamina, having been designed and established, combined, weighed, and changed by God, He formed by them: seven planets in the world, seven days in the year, seven gates, openings of the senses, in man, male and female.

### SECTION 7.

The seven planets in the world are :[36] Saturn, Jupiter, Mars, Sun, Venus, Mercury, Moon. Seven days in the year are the seven days of the week; seven gates in man, male and female, are: two eyes, two ears, two nostrils and the mouth.

### SECTION 8.

FIRST DIVISION. He let the letter ב predominate in wisdom, crowned it, combined one with the other and formed by them: the moon in the world, the first day in the year, and the right eye in man, male and female.

### SECTION 9.

SECOND DIVISION. He let the letter ג predominate in wealth, crowned it, combined one with the other, and formed by them: Mars in the world, the second day in the year, and the right ear in man, male and female.

שִׁבְעָה וְלֹא שְׁמוֹנָה בְּחוֹן בָּהֶם בָּהֶם וַחֲקוֹר בָּהֶם וְהַעֲמֵד
דָּבָר עַל בּוּרְיוֹ וְהוֹשֵׁב יוֹצֵר עַל מְכוֹנוֹ:

## מִשְׁנָה ו.

שֶׁבַע כְּפוּלוֹת בְּגַ״ד כַּפְרַ״ת יְסוֹד חָקְקָן חָצְבָן צָרְפָן
שְׁקָלָן וְהֵמִירָן וְצָר בָּהֶם שִׁבְעָה כּוֹכָבִים בָּעוֹלָם
שִׁבְעָה יָמִים בְּשָׁנָה שִׁבְעָה שְׁעָרִים בְּנֶפֶשׁ זָכָר
וּנְקֵבָה:

## מִשְׁנָה ז.

שִׁבְעָה כּוֹכָבִים בָּעוֹלָם שַׁבְּתַי צֶדֶק מַאֲדִים חַמָּה
נֹגַהּ כּוֹכָב לְבָנָה שִׁבְעָה יָמִים בְּשָׁנָה שִׁבְעָה יְמֵי
הַשָּׁבוּעַ שִׁבְעָה שְׁעָרִים בְּנֶפֶשׁ זָכָר וּנְקֵבָה שְׁתֵּי
עֵינַיִם שְׁתֵּי אָזְנַיִם שְׁנֵי נַקְבֵי הָאַף וְהַפֶּה:

## מִשְׁנָה ח.

בָּבָא א. הִמְלִיךְ אוֹת ב' בְּחָכְמָה וְקָשַׁר לוֹ כֶּתֶר
וְצָרְפָן זֶה בְזֶה וְצָר בָּהֶם לְבָנָה בָּעוֹלָם יוֹם רִאשׁוֹן
בְּשָׁנָה וְעַיִן יָמִין בְּנֶפֶשׁ זָכָר וּנְקֵבָה:

## מִשְׁנָה ט.

בָּבָא ב. הִמְלִיךְ אוֹת ג' בְּעוֹשֶׁר וְקָשַׁר לוֹ כֶּתֶר
וְצָרְפָן זֶה בְזֶה וְצָר בָּהֶם מַאֲדִים בָּעוֹלָם יוֹם שֵׁנִי
בְּשָׁנָה וְאֹזֶן יָמִין בְּנֶפֶשׁ זָכָר וּנְקֵבָה:

## SECTION 10.

THIRD DIVISION. He let the letter ר predominate in producibility, crowned it, combined one with the other, and formed by them: the sun in the world, the third day in the year, the right nostril in man, male and female.

## SECTION 11.

FOURTH DIVISION. He let the letter כ predominate in life, crowned it, combined one with the other, and formed by them: Venus in the world, the fourth day in the year, and the left eye in man, male and female.

## SECTION 12.

FIFTH DIVISION. He let the letter ד predominate in dominion, crowned it, combined one with the other, and formed by them: Mercury in the world, the fifth day in the year, and the left ear in man, male and female.

## SECTION 13.

SIXTH DIVISION. He let the letter ר predominate in peace, crowned it, combined one with the other, and formed by them: Saturn in the world, the sixth day in the year, and the left nostril in man, male and female.

## SECTION 14.

SEVENTH DIVISION. He let the letter ת predominate in beauty, crowned it, combined one with the other, and formed by them: Jupiter in the world, the seventh day in the year, and the mouth of man, male and female.

## מ ש נ ה   י.

בָּבָא ג.. הִמְלִיךְ אוֹת ד׳ בְּזְרוֹעַ וְקָשַׁר לוֹ כֶּתֶר
וְצֵרְפָן זֶה בְזֶה וְצָר בָּהֶם חַמָּה בָּעוֹלָם יוֹם שְׁלִישִׁי
בְּשָׁנָה וּנְחִיר יָמִין בְּנֶפֶשׁ זָכָר וּנְקֵבָה:

## מ ש נ ה   י״א.

בָּבָא ד. הִמְלִיךְ אוֹת כ׳ בְּחַיִּים וְקָשַׁר לוֹ כֶּתֶר
וְצֵרְפָן זֶה בְזֶה וְצָר בָּהֶם נוֹגַהּ בָּעוֹלָם יוֹם רְבִיעִי
בְּשָׁנָה וְעֵין שְׂמֹאל בְּנֶפֶשׁ זָכָר וּנְקֵבָה:

## מ ש נ ה   י״ב.

בָּבָא ה. הִמְלִיךְ אוֹת פ׳ בְּמֶמְשָׁלָה וְקָשַׁר לוֹ כֶּתֶר
וְצֵרְפָן זֶה בְזֶה וְצָר בָּהֶם כּוֹכָב בָּעוֹלָם יוֹם חֲמִישִׁי
בְּשָׁנָה וְאֹזֶן שְׂמֹאל בְּנֶפֶשׁ זָכָר וּנְקֵבָה:

## מ ש נ ה   י״ג.

בָּבָא ו. הִמְלִיךְ אוֹת ר׳ בְּשָׁלוֹם וְקָשַׁר לוֹ כֶּתֶר
וְצֵרְפָן זֶה בְזֶה וְצָר בָּהֶם שַׁבְתַּי בָּעוֹלָם יוֹם שִׁשִּׁי
בְּשָׁנָה וּנְחִיר שְׂמֹאל בְּנֶפֶשׁ זָכָר וּנְקֵבָה:

## מ ש נ ה   י״ד.

בָּבָא ז. הִמְלִיךְ אוֹת ת׳ בְּחֵן וְקָשַׁר לוֹ כֶּתֶר
וְצֵרְפָן זֶה בְזֶה וְצָר בָּהֶם צֶדֶק בָּעוֹלָם יוֹם שַׁבָּת
בְּשָׁנָה וּפֶה בְּנֶפֶשׁ זָכָר וּנְקֵבָה:

## SECTION 15.

By the seven double consonants, בגד כפרת were also designed seven worlds (αιῶνες), seven heavens, seven lands, (probably climates,) seven seas, (probably around Palestine,) seven rivers, seven deserts, seven days a week, seven weeks from Passover to Pentecost, there is a cycle of seven years, the seventh is the release year, and after seven release years is jubilee. Hence, God loves the number seven under the whole heaven.[37] (In the whole nature.)

## SECTION 16.

Two stones build two houses, three stones build six houses, four build twenty-four houses, five build one hundred and twenty houses, six build seven hundred and twenty houses and seven build five thousand and forty[38] houses. From thence further go and reckon what the mouth cannot express and the ear cannot hear.

————

# CHAPTER V.

## SECTION 1.

The twelve simple letters ה״ו״ז ח״ט״י ל״נ״ם ע״צ״ק symbolize, as it were, the organs of speaking, think-

## מִשְׁנָה ט"ו.

שֶׁבַע כְּפוּלוֹת בְּגִי"ד כַּפְרַ"ת שֶׁבָּהֶן נֶחְקְקוּ שִׁבְעָה
עוֹלָמוֹת שִׁבְעָה רְקִיעִין שִׁבְעָה אֲרָצוֹת שִׁבְעָה יַמִּים
שִׁבְעָה נְהָרוֹת שִׁבְעָה מִדְבָּרוֹת שִׁבְעָה יָמִים שִׁבְעָה
שָׁבוּעוֹת שִׁבְעָה שָׁנִים שִׁבְעָה שְׁמִיטִין שִׁבְעָה יוֹבְלוֹת
לְפִיכָךְ חִבֵּב אֶת הַשְּׁבִיעִיּוֹת תַּחַת כָּל הַשָּׁמָיִם:

## מִשְׁנָה ט"ז.

שְׁתֵּי אֲבָנִים בּוֹנוֹת שְׁנֵי בָתִּים שָׁלֹשׁ אֲבָנִים
בּוֹנוֹת שִׁשָּׁה בָתִּים אַרְבַּע אֲבָנִים בּוֹנוֹת אַרְבָּעָה
וְעֶשְׂרִים בָּתִּים חָמֵשׁ אֲבָנִים בּוֹנוֹת מֵאָה וְעֶשְׂרִים
בָּתִּים שֵׁשׁ אֲבָנִים בּוֹנוֹת שְׁבַע מֵאוֹת וְעֶשְׂרִים
בָּתִּים שֶׁבַע אֲבָנִים בּוֹנוֹת חֲמֵשֶׁת אֲלָפִים
(וְאַרְבַּע) וְאַרְבָּעִים בָּתִּים מִכַּאן וָאֵילָךְ צֵא וַחֲשׁוֹב
מַה שֶּׁאֵין הַפֶּה יְכוֹלָה לְדַבֵּר וְאֵין הָאֹזֶן יְכוֹלָה
לִשְׁמֹעַ:

———

# פֶּרֶק חֲמִישִׁי.

## מִשְׁנָה א.

שְׁתֵּים עֶשְׂרֵה פְּשׁוּטוֹת הו"ז חט"י לנ"ס עצ"ק

ing, walking, seeing, hearing, working, coition, smelling, sleep, anger, swallowing and laughing.

## Section 2.

The twelve simple consonants ק"ע ם"נ'ל י"ט"ח ז"ו"ה
symbolize also twelve oblique points: east height,
north east, east depth, south height, south east, south
depth, west height, south west, west depth, north
height, north west, north depth. They grew wider
and wider to all eternity, and these are the boundaries
of the world.

## Section 3.

The twelve simple letters ק"צ"ע ם"נ"יל י"ט"ח ז" י"ה
stamina, having been designed, established, combined, weighed and changed by God, He performed
by them: twelve constellations in the world, twelve
months in the year, and twelve leaders (organs) in the
human body, male and female.

## Section 4.

The twelve constellations in the world are: Aries,

יְסוֹדָן שִׂיחָה הִרְהוּר הִלּוּךְ רְאִיָּה שְׁמִיעָה מַעֲשֶׂה
תַּשְׁמִישׁ רֵיחַ שֵׁנָה רוֹגֶז לְעִיטָה שְׂחוֹק:

### מִשְׁנָה ב.

שְׁתֵּים עֶשְׂרֵה פְּשׁוּטוֹת הו"ז חט"י לנ"ם עצ"ק
יְסוֹדָן שְׁנֵים עָשָׂר גְּבוּלֵי אֲלַכְסוֹן גְּבוּל מִזְרָחִית
רוֹמִית גְּבוּל מִזְרָחִית צְפוֹנִית גְּבוּל מִזְרָחִית תַּחְתִּית
גְּבוּל דְּרוֹמִית רוֹמִית גְּבוּל דְּרוֹמִית מִזְרָחִית גְּבוּל
דְּרוֹמִית תַּחְתִּית גְּבוּל מַעֲרָבִית רוֹמִית גְּבוּל
מַעֲרָבִית דְּרוֹמִית גְּבוּל מַעֲרָבִית תַּחְתִּית גְּבוּל
צְפוֹנִית רוֹמִית גְּבוּל צְפוֹנִית מַעֲרָבִית גְּבוּל צְפוֹנִית
תַּחְתִּית וּמִתְרַחֲבִין וְהוֹלְכִין עַד עֲדֵי עַד וְהֵן הֵן
גְּבוּלוֹת עוֹלָם:

### מִשְׁנָה ג.

שְׁתֵּים עֶשְׂרֵה פְּשׁוּטוֹת הו"ז חט"י לנ"ם עצ"ק
יְסוֹדָן הָקְקָן חָצְבָן הָטְבָן צְרָפָן שְׁקָלָן וְהֵמִירָן וְצָר בָּהֶם
שְׁתֵּים עֶשְׂרֵה מַזָּלוֹת בָּעוֹלָם שְׁנֵים עָשָׂר חֳדָשִׁים
בַּשָּׁנָה שְׁנֵים עָשָׂר מַנְהִיגִים בַּנֶּפֶשׁ זָכָר וּנְקֵבָה:

### מִשְׁנָה ד.

שְׁתֵּים עֶשְׂרֵה מַזָּלוֹת בָּעוֹלָם טָלֶה שׁוֹר תְּאוֹמִים

Taurus, Gemini, Cancer, Leo, Virgo, Libra, Scorpio, Sagitarius, Capricornus, Aquarius and Pisces. The twelve months of the year are: Nisan, Iyar, Sivan, Tamus, Ab, Elul, Tishri, Marcheshvan, Kislev, Teves, Schevat and Adar. The twelve organs of the human body are : two hands, two feet, two kidneys, gall, small intestines, liver, gullet[39] or esophagus, stomach and milt.

### SECTION 5.

### *First Part.*

FIRST DIVISION. God let the letter ה predominate in speaking, crowned it, combined one with the other, and formed by them: Aries (the Ram) in the world, the month Nisan in the year, and the right foot of the human body, male and female.

### SECTION 6.

SECOND DIVISION. He let the letter ו predominate in thinking, crowned it, combined one with the other, and formed by them: Taurus (the Bull) in the world, the month Iyar in the year and the right kidney of the human body, male and female.

### SECTION 7.

THIRD DIVISION. He let the letter ז predominate in walking, crowned it, combined one with the other, and formed by them: Gemini (the Twins) in the world, the month Sivan in the year, and the left foot of the human body, male and female.

סַרְטָן אַרְיֵה בְּתוּלָה מֹאזְנַיִם עַקְרָב קֶשֶׁת גְּדִי דְּלִי

דָּגִים: שְׁנֵים עָשָׂר חֲדָשִׁים בְּשָׁנָה נִיסָן אִיָּיר סִיוָן

תַּמּוּז אָב אֱלוּל תִּשְׁרִי חֶשְׁוָן כִּסְלֵו טֵבֵת שְׁבָט אֲדָר:

שְׁנֵים עָשָׂר מַנְהִיגִים בְּנֶפֶשׁ זָכָר וּנְקֵבָה שְׁתֵּי יָדַיִם

שְׁתֵּי רַגְלַיִם שְׁתֵּי כְּלָיוֹת מָרָה דַקִּין כָּבֵד (קורקבן)

גַּרְגֶּרֶת קֵבָה טָחוֹל:

### מ ש נ ה ה.

בָּבָא א' מֵהָא. הִמְלִיךְ אוֹת ה' בְּשִׂיחָה וְקָשַׁר לוֹ

כֶּתֶר וְצֵרְפָן זֶה בְּזֶה וְצָר בָּהֶם טָלֶה בְּעוֹלָם וְנִיסָן

בְּשָׁנָה וְרֶגֶל יָמִין בְּנֶפֶשׁ זָכָר וּנְקֵבָה:

### מ ש נ ה ו.

בָּבָא ב' מֵהָא. הִמְלִיךְ אוֹת ו' בְּהִרְהוּר וְקָשַׁר לוֹ

כֶּתֶר וְצֵרְפָן זֶה בְּזֶה וְצָר בָּהֶם שׁוֹר בְּעוֹלָם וְאִיָּיר

בְּשָׁנָה וְכוּלְיָא יְמָנִית בְּנֶפֶשׁ זָכָר וּנְקֵבָה:

### מ ש נ ה ז.

בָּבָא ג' מֵהָא. הִמְלִיךְ אוֹת ז' בְּהִלּוּךְ וְקָשַׁר לוֹ

כֶּתֶר וְצֵרְפָן זֶה בְּזֶה וְצָר בָּהֶם תְּאוֹמִים בְּעוֹלָם וְסִיוָן

בְּשָׁנָה וְרֶגֶל שְׂמֹאל בְּנֶפֶשׁ זָכָר וּנְקֵבָה:

### SECTION 8.

*Second Part.*

FIRST DIVISION. He let the letter ח predominate in seeing, crowned it, combined one with the other, and formed by them: Cancer (the Crab) in the world, the month Tamus in the year, and the right hand of the human body, male and female.

### SECTION 9.

SECOND DIVISION. He let the letter ט predominate in hearing, crowned it, combined one with the other, and formed by them: Leo (the Lion) in the world, the month Ab in the year, and the left kidney of the human body, male and female.

### SECTION 10.

THIRD DIVISION. He let the letter י prodominate in working, crowned it, combined one with the other, and formed by them: Virgo (the Virgin) in the world, the month Elul in the year, and the left hand of the human body, male and female.

### SECTION 11.

*Third Part.*

FIRST DIVISION. He let the letter ל predominate in coition, crowned it, combined one with the other, and formed by them: Libra (the Balance) in the world, the month Tishri in the year, and the gall of the human body, male and female.

### SECTION 12.

SECOND DIVISION. He let the letter נ predominate in smelling, crowned it, combined one with the other, and formed by them: Scorpio (the Scorpion) in the world, the month Marcheshvan in the year, and the small intestines of the human body, male and female.

## מ ש נ ה ח.

בָּבָא א׳ מִן הַשְׁנִיָּה. הִמְלִיךְ אוֹת ח׳ בִּרְאִיָּה וְקָשַׁר
לוֹ כֶּתֶר וְצָרְפָן זֶה בָּזֶה וְצָר בָּהֶם סַרְטָן בָּעוֹלָם
וְתַמּוּז בְּשָׁנָה וָיָד יָמִין בְּנֶפֶשׁ זָכָר וּנְקֵבָה:

## מ ש נ ה ט.

בָּבָא ב׳ מִן הַשְׁנִיָּה. הִמְלִיךְ אוֹת ט׳ בִּשְׁמִיעָה
וְקָשַׁר לוֹ כֶּתֶר וְצָרְפָן זֶה בָּזֶה וְצָר בָּהֶם אַרְיֵה בָּעוֹלָם
וְאָב בְּשָׁנָה וְכוּלְיָא שְׂמָאלִית בְּנֶפֶשׁ זָכָר וּנְקֵבָה:

## מ ש נ ה י.

בָּבָא ג׳ מִן הַשְׁנִיָּה. הִמְלִיךְ אוֹת י׳ בְּמַעֲשֶׂה וְקָשַׁר
לוֹ כֶּתֶר וְצָרְפָן זֶה בָּזֶה וְצָר בָּהֶם בְּתוּלָה בָּעוֹלָם
וֶאֱלוּל בְּשָׁנָה וָיָד שְׂמָאל בְּנֶפֶשׁ זָכָר וּנְקֵבָה:

## מ ש נ ה י"א.

בָּבָא א׳ מִן הַשְׁלִישִׁית. הִמְלִיךְ אוֹת ל׳ בְּתַשְׁמִישׁ
וְקָשַׁר לוֹ כֶּתֶר וְצָרְפָן זֶה בָּזֶה וְצָר בָּהֶם מֹאזְנַיִם
בָּעוֹלָם וְתִשְׁרִי בְּשָׁנָה וּמָרָה בְּנֶפֶשׁ זָכָר וּנְקֵבָה:

## מ ש נ ה י"ב.

בָּבָא ב׳ מִן הַשְׁלִישִׁית. הִמְלִיךְ אוֹת נ׳ בְּרֵיחַ וְקָשַׁר
לוֹ כֶּתֶר וְצָרְפָן זֶה בָּזֶה וְצָר בָּהֶם עַקְרָב בָּעוֹלָם
וּמַרְחֶשְׁוָן בְּשָׁנָה וְדַקִין בְּנֶפֶשׁ זָכָר וּנְקֵבָה:

## SECTION 13.

THIRD DIVISION. He let the letter ס predominate in sleep, crowned it, combined one with the other, and formed by them: Sagittarius (the Archer) in the world, the month Kislev in the year, and the stomach of the human body, male and female.

## SECTION 14.

### *Fourth Part.*

FIRST DIVISION. He let the letter ע predominate in anger, crowned it, combined one with the other, and formed by them: Capricornus (the Goat) in the world, the month Teves in the year, and the liver in the human body, male and female.

## SECTION 15.

SECOND DIVISION. He let the letter צ predominate in swallowing, crowned it, combined one with the other, and formed by them: Aquarius (the Water-man) in the world, the month Schwat in the year, and the esophagus of the human body, male and female.

## SECTION 16.

THIRD DIVISION. He let the letter ק predominate in laughing, crowned it, combined one with the other, and formed by them: Pisces (the Fishes) in the world, the month Adar in the year, and the milt of the human body, male and female.

He made them as a conflict, drew them up like a wall; and set one against the other as in warfare.

## מ ש נ ה  י"ג.

בָּכָא ג׳ מִן הַשְּׁלִישִׁית. הִמְלִיךְ אוֹת ס׳ בְּשָׁנָה
וְקָשַׁר לוֹ כֶּתֶר וְצָרְפָן זֶה בָזֶה וְצָר בָּהֶם קֶשֶׁת בְּעוֹלָם
וְכִסְלֵו בְּשָׁנָה וְקֵיבָה בְּנֶפֶשׁ זָכָר וּנְקֵבָה:

## מ ש נ ה  י"ד.

בָּכָא א׳ מִן הָרְבִיעִית. הִמְלִיךְ אוֹת ע׳ בְּרוֹגֶז
וְקָשַׁר לוֹ כֶּתֶר וְצָרְפָן זֶה בָזֶה וְצָר בָּהֶם גְּדִי בְּעוֹלָם
טֵבֵת בְּשָׁנָה וְכָבֵד בְּנֶפֶשׁ זָכָר וּנְקֵבָה:

## מ ש נ ה  ט"ו.

בָּכָא ב׳ מִן הָרְבִיעִית. הִמְלִיךְ אוֹת צ׳ בְּלְעִיטָה
וְקָשַׁר לוֹ כֶּתֶר וְצָרְפָן זֶה בָזֶה וְצָר בָּהֶם דְּלִי בְּעוֹלָם
וּשְׁבָט בְּשָׁנָה (וְקוּרְקְבָן) וְגַרְגֶּרֶת בְּנֶפֶשׁ זָכָר וּנְקֵבָה:

## מ ש נ ה  ט"ז.

בָּכָא ג׳ מִן הָרְבִיעִית. הִמְלִיךְ אוֹת ק׳ בִּשְׂחוֹק
וְקָשַׁר לוֹ כֶּתֶר וְצָרְפָן זֶה בָזֶה וְצָר בָּהֶם דָּגִים בְּעוֹלָם
וַאֲדָר בְּשָׁנָה וּטְחוֹל בְּנֶפֶשׁ זָכָר וּנְקֵבָה עֲשָׂאָן כְּמִין
עֲרֵיכָה׳ סִידְרָן כְּמִין חוֹמָה עָרְכָן כְּמִין מִלְחָמָה:

─────────────

*) נ"א מְרִיבָה אוֹ מְדִינָה:

# CHAPTER VI.

## SECTION 1.

These are the three mothers or the first elements, אמ"ש from which emanated three progenitors; primitive air, water and fire, and from which emanated as their offspring, three progenitors and their offspring, namely: the seven planets and their hosts, and the twelve oblique points.

## SECTION 2.

To confirm this there are faithful witnesses; the world, year and man, the twelve, the Equipoise, the heptade, which God regulates like the Dragon,[40] (Tali) sphere and the heart.

## SECTION 3.

The first elements אמ"ש are air, water and fire; the fire is above, the water below, and a breath of air establishes the balance among them. For an illustration may serve, that the fire carries the water is the phonetic character of מ which is mute and ש is hissing like fire, there is א among them, a breath of air which places them in eqilibrium.[41]

## SECTION 4.

Dragon (Tali) is in the world like a king upon his throne, the sphere is in the year like a king in the empire, and the heart is in the human body like a king[42] in war.

# פרק ששי׃

## מ ש נ ה א.

אֵלּוּ הֵם שָׁלשׁ אִמּוֹת אֶ״מֶ״שׁ וְיָצְאוּ מֵהֶם שְׁלשָׁה אָבוֹת וְהֵם אַוִּיר וּמַיִם וְאֵשׁ וּמֵאָבוֹת תּוֹלְדוֹת שְׁלשָׁה אָבוֹת וְתוֹלְדוֹתֵיהֶם וְשִׁבְעָה כּוֹכָבִים וְצִבְאוֹתֵיהֶם וּשְׁנַיִם עָשָׂר גְּבוּלֵי אֲלַכְסוֹן׃

## מ ש נ ה ב.

רַאֲיָה לַדָּבָר עֵדִים נֶאֱמָנִים בָּעוֹלָם שָׁנָה נֶפֶשׁ וּשְׁנַיִם עָשָׂר חָק וְשִׁבְעָה וּשְׁלשָׁה וּפִקְדָן כְּתָלֵי וְגַלְגַּל וָלֵב׃

## מ ש נ ה ג.

שָׁלשׁ אִמּוֹת אֶ״מֶ״שׁ אַוִּיר אֵשׁ וּמַיִם אֵשׁ לְמַעֲלָה וּמַיִם לְמַטָּה וְאַוִּיר רוּחַ חָק מַכְרִיעַ בְּנְתַּיִם וְסִימָן לַדָּבָר הָאֵשׁ נוֹשֵׂא אֶת הַמַּיִם מִי׳ דוֹמֶמֶת שֶׁ׳ שׁוֹרְקֶת א׳ אַוִּיר רוּחַ חָק מַכְרִיעַ בְּנְתַּיִם׃

## מ ש נ ה ד.

תָּלִי בָּעוֹלָם כְּמֶלֶךְ עַל כִּסְאוֹ גַלְגַּל בְּשָׁנָה כְּמֶלֶךְ בִּמְדִינָה׳ לֵב בְּנֶפֶשׁ כְּמֶלֶךְ בְּמִלְחָמָה׃

---

*) נ״א עַל חוֹמָה׃

## SECTION 5.

God has also set the one over against the other; the good against the evil, and the evil against the good; the good proceeds from the good, and the evil from the evil; the good purifies the bad, and the bad the good; the good is preserved for the good, and the evil for the bad ones.

## SECTION 6.

There are three of which every one of them stands by itself; one is in the affirmative, the other in the negative and one equalizes them.

## SECTION 7.

There are seven of which three are against three, and one places them in equilibrium. There are twelve which are all the time at war; three of them produce love, and three hatred, three are animators and three destroyers.

## SECTION 8.

The three that produce love are the heart and the ears; the three that produce hatred are the liver, the gall and the tongue; the three animators are the two nostrils and the milt; and the three destroyers are the mouth and the two openings of the body; and God, the faithful King, rules over all from His holy habitation to all eternity. He is one above three, three are above seven, seven above twelve, and all are linked together.

## מִשְׁנָה ה.

גַּם אֶת זֶה לְעֻמַּת זֶה עָשָׂה אֱלֹהִים טוֹב לְעֻמַּת
רָע רָע לְעֻמַּת טוֹב טוֹב מִטּוֹב רָע מֵרָע הַטּוֹב
מַבְחִין אֶת הָרָע וְהָרָע מַבְחִין אֶת הַטּוֹב טוֹבָה
שְׁמוּרָה לַטּוֹבִים וְרָעָה שְׁמוּרָה לָרָעִים:

## מִשְׁנָה ו.

שְׁלֹשָׁה כָּל אֶחָד לְבַדּוֹ עוֹמֵד אֶחָד מְזַכֶּה וְאֶחָד
מְחַיֵּיב וְאֶחָד מַכְרִיעַ בְּנְתַּיִם:

## מִשְׁנָה ז.

שִׁבְעָה שְׁלֹשָׁה מוּל שְׁלֹשָׁה וְאֶחָד מַכְרִיעַ בְּנְתַּיִם
וּשְׁנֵים עָשָׂר עוֹמְדִין בַּמִּלְחָמָה: שְׁלֹשָׁה אוֹהֲבִים
שְׁלֹשָׁה שׂוֹנְאִים שְׁלֹשָׁה מְחַיִּים וּשְׁלֹשָׁה מְמִיתִים:

## מִשְׁנָה ח.

שְׁלֹשָׁה אוֹהֲבִים הַלֵּב וְהָאָזְנַיִם שְׁלֹשָׁה שׂוֹנְאִים
הַכָּבֵד הַמָּרָה וְהַלָּשׁוֹן שְׁלֹשָׁה מְחַיִּים שְׁנֵי נִקְבֵי הָאַף
וְהַטְּחוֹל וּשְׁלֹשָׁה מְמִיתִים שְׁנֵי הַנְּקָבִים וְהַפֶּה וְאֵל
מֶלֶךְ נֶאֱמָן מוֹשֵׁל בְּכֻלָּם מִמְּעוֹן קָדְשׁוֹ עַד עֲדֵי עַד
אֶחָד עַל גַּבֵּי שְׁלֹשָׁה שְׁלֹשָׁה עַל גַּבֵּי שִׁבְעָה שִׁבְעָה
עַל גַּבֵּי שְׁנֵים עָשָׂר וְכֻלָּם אֲדוּקִים זֶה בָּזֶה:

## SECTION 9.

There[43] are twenty-two letters by which the I am, Yah, the Lord of hosts, Almighty and Eternal, designed, formed and created by three Sepharim, His whole world, and formed by them creatures and all those that will be formed in time to come.

## SECTION 10.

When[44] the patriarch Abraham comprehended the great truism, revolved it in his mind, conceived it perfectly, made careful investigations and profound inquiries, pondered upon it and succeeded in contemplations, the Lord of the Universe appeared to him, called him his friend, made with him a covenant between the ten fingers of his hands, which is the covenant of the tongue,[45] and the covenant between the ten toes of his feet, which is the covenant of circumcision, and said of him: "Before I formed thee in the belly I knew thee." (Jer. I, 5.)

## מ ש נ ה ט.

אֵלּוּ הֵם עֶשְׂרִים וּשְׁתַּיִם אוֹתִיּוֹת שֶׁבָּהֶן חָקַק אֶהְיֶה
יָהּ יְהֹוָה צְבָאוֹת אֵל שַׁדַּי יְהֹוָה אֱלֹהִים וְעָשָׂה מֵהֶם
שְׁלֹשָׁה סְפָרִים וּבָרָא מֵהֶם אֶת כָּל עוֹלָמוֹ וְצָר בָּהֶם
אֵת כָּל הַיָּצוּר וְאֵת כָּל הֶעָתִיד לָצוּר׃

## מ ש נ ה י.

וּכְשֶׁהֵבִין אַבְרָהָם אָבִינוּ וְהִבִּיט וְרָאָה וְחָקַק וְחָצֵב
וְעָלְתָה בְּיָדוֹ נִגְלָה עָלָיו אֲדוֹן הַכֹּל וְקִרְאוֹ אוֹהֲבִי
וְכָרַת לוֹ בְּרִית בֵּין עֶשֶׂר אֶצְבְּעוֹת יָדָיו וְהוּא בְּרִית
הַלָּשׁוֹן וּבֵין עֶשֶׂר אֶצְבְּעוֹת רַגְלָיו וְהוּא בְּרִית הַמִּילָה
וְקָרָא עָלָיו בְּטֶרֶם אֶצָּרְךָ בַבֶּטֶן יְדַעְתִּיךָ׃

---

\*) נ"א וְקָשַׁר עֶשְׂרִים וּשְׁתַּיִם אוֹתִיּוֹת בִּלְשׁוֹנוֹ וְתָלָה לוֹ אֵת יְסוֹדָן
מָשְׁכָן בְּמַיִם דְּלָקָן כָּאֵשׁ רַעֲשָׁן כְּרוּחַ בְּעָרָן בְּשִׁבְעָה נְהָגָן בִּשְׁתַּיִם עֶשְׂרֵה
מַזָּלוֹת׃

סְלִיק פִּרְקָא. וּסְלִיק סֵפֶר יְצִירָה׃

# NOTES.

1) Our author maintains that there is a first intelligent, self-existing, almighty, eternal ruling cause of all things, and that an everlasting entity produced nonentities by a progression of effects. The divine knowledge, he adds, differs from the human knowledge in such a degree, that it gives existence to all that is. חקק יה ח׳ צבאות is a talmudical expression. (See Treatise Bava Bathra p. 73.) It seems to me, that the author not only wanted to contradict Plato's assertion that the Supreme Being had need of a plan, like the human architect, to conduct the great design, when he made the fabric of the Universe, but also the common belief that God reasons and acts by ideas like a human being. As the prophet Isaiah exclaimed: "Behold! God has no ideas like you, and his ways of acting are not like yours." (Isaiah 55, 8—9.)

2) The number thirty-two is not only the fifth power of two, and the sum of ten units and twenty-two letters, but is also the sum of the first and last letter of the Hebrew Pentateuch, namely: ב 2 and ל 30, equal thirty-two. (See Kusari p. 343, translated into German by Dr. David Cassel.)

3) Paths denote powers, effects, kinds, forms, degrees or stages.

4) These Sepharim or three words of similar expression signify: first, number, calculation or idea; second, the word; third, the writing of the word. The idea, word and writing (of the word), are signs to man for a thing, and is not the thing itself, to the Creator, however, idea, word and writing (of the word) are the thing itself, or as some ancient Rabbis remarked: מחשבה דבור ומעשה הכל הוא דבר אחד בחק״ב״ח׳ "Idea, word and work are one and the same to God." There is an ideal world in the divine intellect, according to which this sensible world was made. The difference between the human and divine manner of thinking admits no comparison.

5) This means to say, that there has not been any matter or hyle existing from all eternity, containing different kinds of primitive atoms or molecules etc., as the Greek philosopher, Anaxagoras, taught, but that all things are the gradual emanations of one everlasting being. This idea is then symbolically explained in the next paragraph.

6) The design of the author is evidently to deduce the proof of the decade from the phenomena in the nature of man, who is generally considered the crown or the final cause of the terrestial creation, and upon whom God vouchsafed two most precious gifts, namely: the articulated word, and the

religious element (spiritual purity). This passage is explained by Isaac
Satanow in his Hebrew Dictionary entitled Sephath Emeth, p. 44, b:

הזה הלשון הוא עט סופר לתולדות השכלים ואבר המוליד
לתולדות החמריים וכל אחד הוא ברית עולם לקיים את האדם
לפליטה נצחית על שתי צלעותיו חמרו וצורתו האי כדאיתריה
The tongue is, as it were, the .וזה בצורתו האי כדאיתריה זה בחמרו
descriptive pen of all the spiritual issues, and the genital parts are the or-
iginators of the corporeal substances. Every one of them is an eternal
covenant in order to preserve the human race for ever, according to its two-
fold being: body and spirit. Each working after its own way, physically
and spiritually.

7) Like Pythagoras, who taught that the digits inclusive number ten
which are typified in Tetraktys, ($\mathit{Ter\rho\alpha\kappa\tau\upsilon\varsigma}$) namely: 1 plus 2 plus 3
plus 4 equal 10, and which comprise the whole arithmetical system of
nature, etc. Our author endeavors to show the gradual emanation of all
things from God, which were completely finished in ten spheres.

8) My Hebrew reading is: והושב יוצר על מכונו There are various
readings; therefore Postellus rendered it: "restitue figmentum in locum
suum;" Rittangel, "restitue formatorem in throno suo;" Pistorius, "fac
sedere creatorem in throno suo." The author seems to ridicule here the
Gnosticians who maintained that Demiurg was the creator of man and the
sensual world.

9) In God is the beginning and he is the boundary of the Universe.
Compare also the Talmud treatise Chagigah p. 12.

10) Here is contradicted the system of ditheism, consisting of an eternal
God, the Author of all good and of "Hyle" or "Satan," the co-eternal and
co-equal principle of evil, maintaining that an all-perfect God alone is the
author of all good and evil, and has in his infinite wisdom so wonderfully
contrived the nature of things, that physical and moral evil may produce
good, and hence contribute to carry out the great design of the Supreme
Being. Compare also Chap. 6 §5.

11) As the infinite series of numbers starts from one unit, so was the
whole Universe formed a unity, that centres in the Godhead.

12) The meaning is, that as the living creatures which the prophet saw
in his vision were stricken with such an awe, that they could not go any
further to see the divine glory, and had to return, so is the decade an eternal secret to us and we are not permitted to understand it. We find this
very idea in the Pythagorean system. The disciples of Pythagoras looked
upon the decade as a holy number, and swore by it and by the Tetraktys
which contain the number ten.

13) See above Note 1, God, idea and word are indivisible.

14) I adopted here the reading of Judah Halevi, namely: חקק וחצב בהן בהו רפש וטיט וגו׳, with the exception of the word תהו; because it is obvious from "Yezirah," Chap. II, that the author signifies by the word "Tohu," nothing, and not something, as Judah Halevi erroneously thought. Moses Butarel and others tell us that they had before them a correct copy of "Sepher Yezirah," where it reads: תהו זה קו קו ירוק וכו׳ בהו אלו אבנים מפולמות. The same passage is mentioned in the Talmud treatise Chagigah, p. 12, a, with the addition of המשוקעות בתהום שמהן יוצאין מים. The word המפולמות is translated by Rashi, *moist*. Some say it is a compound word of מפול מות, others of פלוני אלמוני, etc. But the word is not of Semitic origin; it is, according to my opinion, borrowed from the Greek as the word סרמן, etc., Πλήμη *flood*. אבנים מפלמות flood-stones. The same word is used treatise Beza, p. 24, b, דגים המפולמין, fish that are caught from out of the flood.

15) According to the author, the space and six dimensions emanated from the ether.

16) Judah Halevi in his book entitled "Kusari," p. 356, illustrates it thus: The Creator is one, and the space has in the figurative expression six dimensions. The book "Yezirah," having ascribed to the Creator some names in the spiritual language, chooses now in the human language the finest sounds which are, as it were, the spirits of the other sounds, namely: "הוי" and says, that when the divine will was expressed by such a sublime name, it became that which the Exalted by praise wished to call forth according to the combination of "הוי," Hence it follows, that the material world was created in such a way and manner which corresponds with the material, namely, by the sublime spiritual name, which corresponds with the material name, יהו׳ והו׳ הוי׳ היו׳ ויה׳ והי׳ and out of each of them became one dimension of the world, the sphere.

17) The author shows here by the symbol of a scale and the phonetic character of the fundamental letters א׳׳מ׳׳ש that the opposite forces and the struggle which prevail in the smallest as well as in the largest circles of creation are appeased and calmed.

18) Meaning outlets, outgates of the creative power, formations.

19) The word ענג signifies joy, and when transposed, forming the word נגע it signifies just the contrary, trouble, plague. He means to say, that the letters of the words ענג and נגע are the same, but they signify nevertheless, opposite ideas on account of transposition. Just as the sphere remains the same during the rotation on its axis in its setting and in its rising; yet it appears to us as if it had undergone a great change on account of its different position.

20) My reading is : צָרְפָן שָׁקְלֵן וְהֵמִירָן׃

21) The combination of the twenty-two letters without permutation is represented in the following table:

22) The number of combinations of twenty-two letters two and two without any permutation is according to the mathematical formula

$$n \cdot \frac{n-1}{2} = 22 - 1 \times \frac{22}{2} = 231.$$

23) The ancient philosophers maintained that if God is the first cause, and He is necessarily, He, the immediate effect of Him, as an absolute unity,

can only be again a unity. Hence from a being that is in every respect a unique being, there can only emanate one being; because would two essentially and truly different things issue conjointly from one being, they can only proceed from two different things of substance, that would consequently admit a division that is inconceivable. They then put the question, how came so many various beings into existence? Our author is therefore endeavoring to show that the whole universe emanated gradually from the spirit of the one living God.

24) The reading of Von Jo. Meyer and others is as follows: רצר מתודו ממש ועשח אינו רשנו והצב עמודים גדולים מאודר שאינו נחפס וזה סימן צופה ומימר עושח כל היצור ואת כל הדברים בשם אחד וסימן לדבר עשרים ושתים מנירנם דגוף אחד: My reading according to a manuscript of Rabbi Isaac Luria, which I have preferred to all others, is thus: רצר ממש מתודו ועשה את אינו רשנו והצב עמודים גדולים מאודר שאינו נחפס וזה סימן אות א עם כולן וכולן עם א צופה ומימר ועשח את כל היצור ואת כל הדבור שם אחד וסימן לדבר עשרים ושתים חפצים בגוף א:

25) It has been already mentioned above Chap. i, §1, that God, his idea and his word are a unity; hence the author signifies by the letter Aleph the air from which emanated the creative speech, etc.

26) Here is meant: ethereal air, ethereal water, ethereal fire, the macrocosm, the courses of time and microcosm. Many offspring or derivations came from the latter three, as their progenitors, as it is explained afterwards in the chapter.

27) The author endeavors to show how the creative divine word became more condensed and how a new series of productions came out of three elements.

28) In ancient times coldness was considered to oe a substance. [See Psalm 147, 17.]

29) Id est, made it the reigning power.

30) Namely, with the two other elements.

31) That is to say a different combination of the elements.

32) According to the opinion of the author, it may be arranged as follows:

|        | Aleph.    | Mem.                            | Sheen.               |
|--------|-----------|---------------------------------|----------------------|
| World: | Air,      | Earth,<br>(Inclusive of Land and Sea.) | Heaven or Atmosphere. |
| Man:   | Breast,   | Belly,                          | Head.                |
| Year:  | Moistness, | Coldness,                      | Heat.                |

33) The aspirating pronunciation of ρ in the Greek, was adopted by the ancient Jews in Palestine for the Hebrew letter ר. They pronounced it partly aspirated and partly unaspirated. [See Dr. Geiger's Lehr-und Lesebuch der Mischnah, p. 22, and Dr. Graetz's Gnosticismus, p. 117.]

34) According to the idea of our author, there emanated from the unity of God three ethereal elements: primitive air from the spirit, from the air, primitive water, and from the water, primitive fire or ether, out of which came other spheres of existence in the significant and highly important number, seven, from which descended smaller spheres and which produced again others. He endeavors to show how the ideal became, after numerous emanations, more condensed, palpable and concrete. The whole creation is thus contemplated as a pyramid, terminating in a point at the top with a broad basis. [See Dr. Graetz's Gnosticismus, p. 224.]

35) Compare Chapter I, Section 3, Note, 8.

36) The order of the planets (including the Sun) is stated here according to the Ptolemaic system which was in vogue even among the learned men till the middle of the fifteenth century, namely: Moon, Mercury, Venus, Sun, Mars, Jupiter and Saturn. But this arrangement is undoubtedly an interpolation of a later time, as the author of the book "Yezirah" lived many years before Ptolemy. And indeed Prof. Jo. Friedrich Von Meyer and others of reliable authority had in their copies of "Yezirah" the following order: חמה נוגה כוכב לבנה שבתי צדק מאדים, Mars, Jupiter, Saturn, Moon, Mercury, Venus, Sun.

37) Philo (Allegor 1, 42,) after having called attention to the fact that the heptade is to be found in many biblical laws, in the vowels of the Greek language, in the gamut and in the organs of the human body, exclaims, similar to our author: "The whole nature exults in the heptade!"

38) The rule for permutation is as follows: (n—1). n. 1 x 2 x 3 x 4 x 5 x 6 x 7=5040. In our edition it reads: חמשת אלפים וארבע בתים, Five thousand and four houses, which is obviously a mistake, it should read: 5040 houses. חמשת אלפים וארבעים בתים

39) I read גרגרת instead of קורקובן for two reasons. In the first place, the same thing is mentioned afterwards, and in the second place, it is proved by the expression לפרסה that the author meant גרגרת and not קורקובן.

40) Some maintain that by the expression Tali is understood the constellation Draco or Dragon, which is a very large constellation extending for a great length from East to West; beginning at the tail which lies half way between the Pointers and the Pole Star, and winding round between the Great and Little Bear by a continued succession of bright stars from 5 to 10 degrees asunder, it coils round under the feet of the Little Bear, sweeps round the pole of the ecliptic, and terminates in a trapezium formed by four conspicuous stars from 30 to 35 degrees from North Pole. Dr. Steinshneider (see Magazin fuer Literatur des Auslandes, 1845) and Dr. Cassel (in his commentary to the book entitled Kusari,) maintain that the ancient Jewish

astronomers signified by the word Tali, not the constellation Draco, but the line which joins together the two points in which the orbit of the moon intercepts the ecliptic (Dragon's head and tail). Dr. Cassel is of the opinion that our author meant here, probably the invisible, celestial or universal axis that carries the whole Universe.

41) Our author means to say that the water has a great disposition to unite itself with the caloric, thus for instance is the fire latent in steam, but the air equipoises them.

42) The meaning is, as God is the centre of the Universe, so have the macrocosm, the seasons and temperature and the microcosm, their centres receiving power from the principal centre to regulate and rule.

43) The substance of this Mishnah is mentioned in the Talmud treatise Berachoth, p. 55, a. It reads there: אמר רב יהודה אמר רב יודע היה בצלאל לצרף אותיות שנבראו בהן שמים וארץ׃ "Rab Jehudah stated in the name of Rab, that Bezalel understood to combine letters by which heaven and earth were created." To this the commentator Rashi adds: "as it is taught in the book Yezirah." It is undoubtedly certain that the book Yezirah, or a cosmogony as it is represented there, was known to Rab, who was a disciple of Jehudah Hanasi, during the second part of the second century. (C. E.) See treatise Berachoth, p. 55 a, where the commentator Rashi referred to the book Yezirah.

44) This whole paragraph is an interpolation of an unknown hand, as it can be easily proved.

45) I have translated according to the reading of Rabbi Judah Halevi. The reading of Rabbi Luria is as follows: וקשר עשרים ושתים אותיות בלשונו וגילה לו את סודו משכן במרים דלקן באש רעשן ברוח בערן בשבעה מהגין בשנים עשר מזלות׃ "He fastened twenty-two letters on his tongue and revealed to him His mystery, He drew them by water, kindled them by fire and thundered them by the wind, He lighted them by seven, and rules them by twelve constellations." Pistor. renders it: "Tranat per aquam, accendit in igne grandine signavit in äere. Disposuit cum septem et gubernavit cum duodecim." Postellus' version is: "Attraxit eum in aqua, accendit in spiritu, inflammavit in septem aptatum cum duodecim signis." Meyer translates it: "Er zog sie mit Wasser, zündet sie an mit Feuer, erregte sie mit Geist, vebrannte sie mit sieben, goss sie aus mit den zwoelf Gestirnen."

# GLOSSARY

## OF

# RABBINICAL WORDS.

---

## א

| אָדַק | *v.* | To adhere, cohere. VI, 8. |
| אֲוִיר | *n.* | [Syriac, אאר, Greek ἀήρ] Air. II, .. |
| אוֹת | *n.* | Sign, letter; אוֹתִיּוֹת יְסוֹד fundamental letters. I, 1. |
| אֵילָךְ | *adv.* | מִכָּאן וְאֵילָךְ hinc et ulterius; from now further. IV 16 |
| אֵלּוּ | *adj.* | These. Equals the biblical אֵלֶּה. VI, 1. |
| אֲלַכְסָן | *adj.* | [Greek λόξον] Oblique, diagonal direction. V, 2. |
| אֶמְצַע | *n.* | Middle. centre. I, 2. |

## ב

| בֵּרוּי | *n.* | Clearness, perspicuity. I, 3. וְהֶעֱמֵד דָּבָר עַל בֵּרוּיוֹ and put the subject in a clear point of view. |
| בְּבָא | *n.* | Division. V, 5. |
| בֵּינוֹתַיִם *or* בְּנָתַיִם | | Composed of בֵּין שְׁתַּיִם, omitting שֶׁ between them. I, 1. [See Duke's Sprache der Mischnah. p. 68.] |

## ג

| גַּב | \*n.* | Back. עַל גַּבֵּי upon the back id est, upon or above. VI, 8. |
| גוּף | *n.* | Body, substance II, 5. |
| גַּלְגַּל | *n.* | Circle, celestial orb, or sphere. II, 4. |

## ד

| | | |
|---|---|---|
| דִּבּוּר | n. | Word. I, 8. |

## ה

| | | |
|---|---|---|
| הִרְהֵר | v. | Think, muse, meditate, reflect. I, 7. |
| הִרְהוּר | n. | Reflection, meditotion. V, 1. |

## ו

| | | |
|---|---|---|
| זְכוּת | n. | Innocence, purity, godliness, merit. II, 1. |

## ח

| | | |
|---|---|---|
| חוֹבָה | n. | Misdeed, trespass. II, 1. |
| חָזַר | v. | To return, to turn one's self round. II, 5. |
| חֲלִילָה | n. | Rotation; from חָלַל to dance round. II, 5. |

## מ

| | | |
|---|---|---|
| טָחוֹל | n. | Milt, spleen. V, 4. |

## כ

| | | |
|---|---|---|
| כָּאן or כַּאן | adv. | Here, there; מִכַּאן thence, from thence. IV, 16. |
| כּוֹכָב | n. | Star; especially the planet Mercury. IV, 7. |
| כֵּן piel כָּן | v. | Direct; מְכֻוָּן directed, situated. I, 2. |
| כִּיעוּר | n. | Ugliness. IV, 3. |
| כָּךְ or לְכָךְ | adv. | So, thus. I, 7. |
| כָּרַע Hiph. הִכְרִיעַ | v. | To intervene in any thing, to mediate the peace, accomodate a quarrel. II, 1. |

## ל

| | | |
|---|---|---|
| לְעִיטָה | n. | Eating, swallowing. V, 1. |
| לְפִיכָךְ | adv. | Composed of the words לְפִי and כָּךְ. According to that, therefore. IV, 15. |

## מ

| | | |
|---|---|---|
| מַאֲדִים | n. | The planet Mars. IV, 7. |
| מִדָּה | n. | Measure, quality, divine attribute. I, 4. |
| מִשְׁנָה | n. | Doctrine, lesson, paragraph. |
| מַזָּלוֹת | n. | Constellations; especially the twelve signs of the Zodiac. V, 3. מַזָּל טוֹב a happy constellation. |
| כְּמִין | adv. | It is a particle like כ, as; it is added the word מִין kind, denoting: as a kind of, like, as. II, 4. |
| מֵימַר | v. | Chald. inf. מֵאמַר or מֵמַר. To speak, command. II, 5. |
| מַמָּשׁ | n. | Substance, reality. II, 5. |
| מַעֲזִיבָה | n. | Rampart, a floor, pavement. I, 8. |
| מָרָה | n. | Gall. V, 4 |
| מִתְנַהֵג | | See נָהַג. IV, 1. |

## נ

| | | |
|---|---|---|
| נָהַג | v. | With a ב following after it, signifies: to make use of any thing. IV, 1. |
| נוֹנַה | n. | The planet Venus. IV, 7. |
| נָעַץ | v. | Chald. Stick in, fasten, conjoin, connect. I, 6. |
| נֶקֶב | n. | Opening. IV, 8. |

## ס

| | | |
|---|---|---|
| סָדַר | v. | Arrange. V, 16. |
| סִימָן | n. | σημεῖον Sign, illustration. II, 4. [See Geiger's Lesestücke der Mishnah, p. 121.] |
| סָלִיק | n. | Finished; the end (of a book or chapter.) |

## ע

| | | |
|---|---|---|
| עֲרִיבָה | n. | Contention, rivalry. V, 5. |
| עָתִיד | n. | Future. II, 2. |

## פ

| | | |
|---|---|---|
| פֶּרֶק | *n.* | Chapter, section. |
| פָּשׁוּט | *adj.* | Divested of clothes, undressed, simple. I, 8. |

## צ

| | | |
|---|---|---|
| צֶדֶק | *n.* | The planet Jupiter. IV, 7. |
| צְמִייַח | *n.* | Appearance. I, 5. |
| צָרַף | *v.* | Refine, melt together, connect, combine. II, 2. |

## ק

| | | |
|---|---|---|
| קָבַע | *v.* | To fix, to fasten. I, 8. II, 3. |
| קֵיבָה *or* קֵבָה | *n.* | Stomach. V, 4. |
| קוּרְקְבָן *or* קֻרְקְבָן | *n.* | Stomach. V, 4. |

## ר

| | | |
|---|---|---|
| רְאָיָה | *n.* | Argument, evidence. VI, 2. |
| רְאִיָּה | *n.* | Sight. V, 1. |
| רְוִיָּה | *n.* | Redundancy of water, moistness. III, 4. |
| רֵיחַ | *v.* | Smell. V, 1. |

## ש

| | | |
|---|---|---|
| שַׁבְתַאי | *n.* | The planet Saturn. IV, 7. |
| שִׂיחָה | *n.* | Speaking. V, 1. |
| שְׁמִיעָה | *n.* | Hearing. V, 1. |
| שֵׁרַת | *v.* | To serve. I, 8. |

## ת

| | | |
|---|---|---|
| תְּלִי | *n.* | The constellation Draco or Dragon. VI, 2. |
| תַשְׁמִישׁ | *n.* | Coition. V, 1. |
| תָּפַס *or* תָּפַשׂ | *v.* | To seize, to take hold of. |

# SEPHER YETZIRAH

ATTRIBUTED BY
## RABBI AKIBA BEN JOSEPH

TRANSLATED FROM THE HEBREW, WITH
ANNOTATIONS, BY
## KNUT STENRING

INCLUDING
## THE 32 PATHS OF WISDOM
THEIR CORRESPONDENCE WITH THE HEBREW ALPHABET
AND THE TAROT SYMBOLS

WITH AN INTRODUCTION BY
## ARTHUR EDWARD WAITE

# Master Key to the Cabala

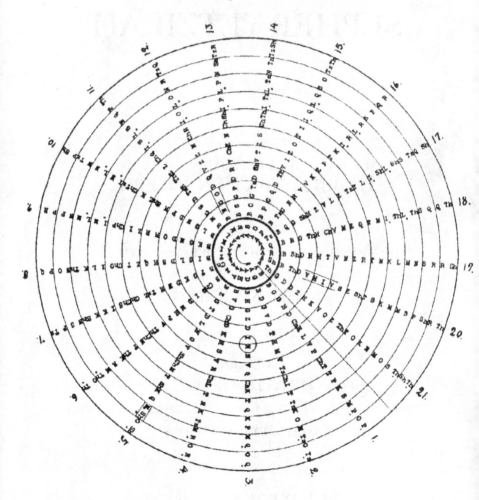

# INTRODUCTION

## By ARTHUR EDWARD WAITE

The SEPHER YETZIRAH is a very small, indeed a minute work, even in its most extended recension; but in the hands of successive translators and makers of commentaries its critical position has become exceedingly complex, and it is scarcely possible to reach, much less to hold, any definite view as a mean between the conflicting elements of debate. For the purpose of the present brief consideration I can assume no knowledge on the part of readers and must present therefore only the simpler issues of the subject.

The SEPHER YETZIRAH, otherwise BOOK OF FORMATION, was introduced to Christian scholarship in 1552 by a Latin translation of William Postel, this being ten years prior to the first issue of the printed Hebrew text, which took place at Mantua in 1562. A second Latin rendering belongs to the year 1587, when it appeared in the first and only volume of ARTIS CABALISTICÆ SCRIPTORES under the editorship of Pistorius. Finally, so far as I am aware, the Hebrew text with a third translation into Latin was produced by Rittangelius in 1642, together with a commentary on THE 32 PATHS OF WISDOM by Rabbi Abraham ben Dior. The translation of the SEPHER was the work of the editor and was accompanied by notes. As regards the Hebrew text, that of Mantua contained two recensions, with variant readings of both, the second being longer than the first. On the one hand, its additional matter is regarded as later interpolation, but on the other it is held to give " valuable readings which seem older and better than corresponding passages in the shorter." This is on the authority of the JEWISH ENCYCLOPÆDIA, vol. xii, *s.v. Yezirah.* Other editions of the Hebrew text—apart from translation—were published : (1) at Amsterdam, in 1642, and again in 1718 ; (2) at Lemberg, in 1680, containing six codices, that of Saadya Gaon included ; (3) at Constantinople, 1719 ; (4) at Zolkiew, in 1745 ; (5) at

Korzec, in 1779, under the editorship of Moses ben Jacob;
(6) at Grodno, in 1806, accompanied by five commentaries;
(7) at Dyhernfurth, in 1812; (8) at Salonika, in 1831; (9) at
Jerusalem, in 1874; (10) at Warsaw, in 1884, with nine
commentaries. It may be added that the bibliography of the
work is not exhausted by this representative enumeration.

Among renderings into modern languages with which I
am acquainted the first in point of time is that of Meyer into
German, together with the Hebrew text, in 1886. In 1894 the
text of Isaac Loria and the text of an Arabic version were
edited by L. Goldschmidt, with a new German translation.
The first French rendering was made by Gérard Encausse,
better known under his pseudonym of Papus. The second was
by Mayer Lambert, in 1891, an elaborate work, containing
(1) the Arabic text of Saadya Gaon's commentary on the
SEPHER YETZIRAH, its translation into French and a rendering
of the SEPHER from the Hebrew. In 1913 the Comtesse Calomira
de Cimara produced a new rendering which was done with
considerable care and was accompanied by folding diagrams
and notes.

The first English translation appeared at New York in
1877, together with the Hebrew text from an excellent fount
of type. It is accompanied by notes of considerable interest
and is followed by A SKETCH OF THE TALMUD. The translator
and author is Mr Isidor Kalisch. The second version is that
of Dr W. Wynn Westcott, published originally in 1887 and
reissued in a revised form, with additional notes, by the
Theosophical Publishing Society as a volume of COLLECTANEA
HERMETICA in 1893. It is based on the text of Rittangelius,
compared with some other versions. It was prepared for the
use of persons described as theosophists, occult and Hermetic
students, whose purpose—if any—may have been served by
such a production, but it is in reality a paraphrase and fulfils
few of the conditions required by scholarship.

As stated in the Translator's Note, the present version is a
word-for-word rendering, the work of a Swedish Hebraist.
It may be compared with the beginnings of a rendering by
Mr Phineas Mordell in his " Origin of Letters and Numerals,
according to the SEFER YETZIRAH," reprinted in Germany from
the JEWISH QUARTERLY REVIEW of 1912–13, and published in
Philadelphia by the author. It is dated 1914, but it is explained
on a slip that no copies of the thesis became available in America
until 1921, owing to the Great War. Mr Mordell's remarkable

study, to which I shall recur shortly, contains the Hebrew text
and parallel English rendering of twenty-four *mishnayoth*,
versicles or paragraphs, to which number his principles of
criticism reduce the original and only authentic text.

Mr Knut Stenring makes clear his personal position by
printing those portions which he believes to be of later date in
italics throughout, and this has the merit of offering a clear
issue to the general reader.

The cosmology of SEPHER YETZIRAH, however we elect to
translate individual words and paragraphs, is the primary concern of the tract, while the second exhibits a correspondence
between the work of God in the universe and in the body of
man, in which connection it is to be observed that there is no
intimation concerning a spiritual part which answers to the
notion of a human soul. The word Formation suggests a work
performed on antecedently existing material, *e.g.*, the " formless
and void " or " mire and clay " of c. I, 11. The Yetziratic Lord
corresponds therefore to the Masonic description of Deity as
the Great Architect of the Universe. It is said indeed in the
text—*ibidem*—that he " hewed " the twenty-two letters " as a
wall " and " covered them as a building." But those who
devised the Emblematic Art *post* 1717 did not intend to suggest
that their Architect was not also Creator, and in like manner
the SEPHER YETZIRAH represents the Lord, God and Holy One,
not only as writing and forming, not only as producing from
void and chaos, but according to Dr Stenring's rendering " He
made the non-existent exist " (II, 6), which is in substantial
agreement with other modern versions. Compare (1) La
Comtesse Cimara : *Il forma quelque chose de concret du Tohu et
fit ce qui n'etait pas.* (2) Dr Wynn Westcott : " From the non-
existent He made something " (II, 5). (8) Mr Phineas Mordell :
" He graved and hewed out of them void and chaos. . . . He
formed existence out of void, and made something out of
nothing " (pars. 19, 22).

The SEPHER YETZIRAH introduces also a doctrine of the
Logos. The universe was created by " three forms of expression
—Numbers, Letters and Words " (Stenring), otherwise by
" Numbers, Letters and Sounds " (Westcott), or by three
" books," which are " Writing, Number and Speech " (Cimara),
for which Mordell substitutes " Scribe, Script and Scroll."
The root and meaning are one in respect of all the variants,
as will be seen more fully by comparing the alternatives of
Postel, Pistorius and Rittangelius, which are cited by Mr

Stenring in his notes. It is said further that the Word of God is in the Sephiroth (I, 6), otherwise Numerations or Digits (Mordell); that Voice, Spirit and Word are together the Spirit of the Holy One (I, 9); that creation as it is and all creation to come are already or will be formed by the twenty-two letters (II, 2); that Air, Water and Fire proceeded from the Three Mother Letters, *Aleph, Mem* and *Shin*; that the seven planets were brought forth from the Seven Double Letters, as also the directions of space and that Holy Palace in the centre which sustains all things (IV, 4, 15), an allusion to the Divine Immanence operating in created things as an unmanifest behind the manifest ; and that the zodiacal signs were drawn forth from the Twelve Simple Letters (V, 3). We may compare later Zoharic doctrine, according to which the letters had been emanated one from another and thereafter the world was created by their help, that it might manifest the Divine Name as an Indwelling Presence therein. Yet later Kabalism distinguished three operations, to create, to form and to make, corresponding to the respective offices of three worlds—*Olam Briah, Olam Yetzirah* and *Olam Assiah*—in the Sephirotic scheme of the Tree of Life, these depending from *Olam Atziluth*, the world of Deity, wherein is the Crown of the Tree.

The SEPHER YETZIRAH unfolds also a logical doctrine of correspondences which was destined to be extended by the ZOHAR and its commentators and connections in several suggestive directions. It is obvious, and as they were men of subtle understanding it must have been realised by the theosophists of Israel that they were setting forth in reality and projecting on the Divine Plane a philosophy of the human Logos. It was man and no other for whom the Ten Numerations were a mode of the rational mind ; it was he who conceived and gave utterance to letters as sounds, in throat, palate and tongue, through teeth and lips (II, 3). His is the science of numbers and his are the forms of speech : it is he who is scribe and script, and there is even a true sense in which he is also the scroll, or that *tabula* on which the cosmos without impresses its messages, to be received and interpreted by the cosmos within. The sacramental correspondence between that which is communicated to the senses and conveyed through these to the mind is like the covenant placed by the Lord between the hands of Abraham (VI, 16), a guarantee on the part of God that there is a valid relation between *signum* and *signatum*, according to the proportion of which the human understanding is an authentic measure of the universe. Mr Stenring places VI, 16, among the apocryphal paragraphs, and Mr Mordell regards it as belonging to the original text. The former in his translation presents Abraham as contemplating, studying and at length understanding the Yetziratic revelation. He " formed and designed till he had reached " this end. On the other hand, according to Mr Mordell, who follows I know not which recension, " when Abraham our father arose, he looked and saw and investigated and observed and engraved and hewed and combined and formed and calculated, and his creation was successful." In other words, by a deep contemplation of the cosmos it was so unfolded to the patriarch that its true pattern was created or formulated in his mind, the result of which (*ibid.*) was that the Lord appeared or was revealed to him, meaning that God became known in His works. Our version says that thereafter " he had faith in the Lord "—because, I conclude, his deep observation of the universe had empowered him to " justify the ways of God to men."

It may well be that this experimental essay in the elucidation of an obscure passage is not precisely according to the mind of the Hebrews, but there is no other in which it can be said of Abraham that " his creation was successful," and it does exhibit the law of correspondence in its most deep aspect. For the rest, according to SEPHER YETZIRAH, the Hebrew Letters which correspond in the macrocosm to Air, Water and Fire answer in the microcosm of man to head, belly and chest (III, 7); the Double Letters which produced the seven planets are in analogy with seven gateways, so called, in the human organism, namely, eyes, ears, nostrils and mouth, the channels of communication from without inward by sight, hearing, smell and taste (IV, 6, 7 *et seq.*). So also the celestial zodiac was produced by means of the Twelve Simple Letters, which are in correspondence also, and after the same manner, with twelve organs—external and internal—of the human economy—hands, feet, stomach and so onward (V, 3, 6 *et seq.*). I suppose that a Kabalistic astrology could be unfolded from this highly symbolical thesis, and something of the kind may have been attempted in recent days.

Mr Stenring has produced his translation for the same reason that actuated Dr Papus and subsequently Dr Westcott : it was supposed then and is supposed now to be of importance for occult students. Based on a better understanding of SEPHER YETZIRAH, Mr Stenring looks for a revival of the whole subject. In the introduction to his translation Dr Westcott points out

that the text is " an instructive philosophical treatise upon one
aspect of the origin of the universe and mankind," to say which,
however, explains nothing respecting the nature of its appeal
to occult students, besides being quite inapplicable as a description of the work itself.  On the other hand, Mr Stenring produces
his reasons for the faith that is in him.  For him the numbers
and letters which make up the Paths of Wisdom represent
forces created by God from which everything was and is formed
in the universe, and by means of their symbols these forces
become apprehensible to the mind (pp. 36, 37).  Moreover, the
work of contemplation can increase knowledge of the forces,
up to a certain point.  Mr Stenring gives further an elaborate
diagram shewing concentric circles inscribed with the English
equivalents of the Hebrew letters arranged in a certain order as
an explanation of Cap. II, 5, in the text.  He claims that this is
the great Kabalistic Symbol and " Master-Key to the theoretical
and practical Kabalah," which the SEPHER YETZIRAH conceals
in a riddle at the place just indicated and which he has been
the first to solve.  It follows that Mr Stenring " delivers the
goods " that were not apparently in the hands of Papus, Westcott
et hoc genus, and therefore occult students who are drawn
towards Jewish symbolism, according to which the Lord wrote
numbers and letters, thus creating forces for the production of
the manifest world, can set to work on his diagram and see
what they can make of it.  They will come at least across many
curious permutations and will be in agreement with myself that
the elaborate Diagram is one of considerable interest, from
whatever point of view it is approached, and however they
may interpret Mr Stenring's statement that absolute knowledge
of a single number or letter is " impossible for a human mind "
(p. 37), unless it has opened every Gate of Understanding,
i.e., has acquired " an encyclopædic knowledge of all sciences."

The early students and editors of SEPHER YETZIRAH—Postel,
Pistorius and Rittangelius—hoped that their own zeal would
effect the conversion of Israel to the faith of Christ, and it is
useful to contrast this enthusiasm with the various motives
which actuate " occult interest " at the present day.  The
Sephirotic and Alphabetical Theosophy of the Yetziratic
Midrash was developed in the ZOHAR, and this storehouse of
Kabalism was in turn developed into a formal system by
rabbinical devotees of the sixteenth and seventeenth centuries.
The system and its sources, being capable of several construc-
tions, were adapted—as I have explained previously on more

than one occasion—by Christian students, from Mirandula to Baron von Rosenroth, for the purpose of proving to Israel that their expected Messiah had come already in Christ. I have shewn also that the informal association for the propagation of the Gospel in the foreign parts of Jewry proved practically of no effect, though the ZOHAR itself must be credited with the conversion of one little band of zealots under Jacob Frank. The occult interest in the SEPHER YETZIRAH is part of the concern in Jewish tradition at large and in other assumed channels of secret knowledge. From my own point of view, it is too often misdirected and therefore loses its way, amidst speculations in cloud and mist on themes which can be hardly specified. There are great masters somewhere about, encompassed by the reverence of pronouns printed with great initial letters; there is a grand secret of undeclared quality hypothecated at the end of a long vista; while if anything can be brought to book in the present connection it is a tentative belief in the question of occult virtue resident in Divine Names. Under such auspices there is no need to add that in Victorian days, when we heard of Hermetic Orders, Brotherhoods of Luxor and the Veil of Isis, it was apt to be a cloak for every kind of false pretence, not to speak of imbecility of thought.

Mr Stenring belongs to another category and is probably concerned with the occult subject as a curious path of research, much as on my own part I devoted years to its study, seeking a possible light on the several lines of development followed by the Secret Tradition in Christian Times. Magia, Theosophia, Alchimia, Kabalah, Philosophia Occulta are or may be among the paths thereof, in an ascending or descending scale. There is valuable work which remains to be done in all, and this is the direction in which we may share the translator's hope for " a much-needed renaissance of occultism." It seems to me that at the present day it has entered into its proper sphere as a study of the records of the past, sometimes in the hope that they may throw incidental light upon modern problems which are grouped together under the denomination of psychical research. Outside this, the pursuit is mainly archæological.

In my DOCTRINE AND LITERATURE OF THE KABALAH, 1902, I indicated that we do not get much help in the study of SEPHER YETZIRAH from the work of modern scholarship which is not of the occult kind, and it is obvious from what has been said that the latter is no source of light. Even at this day the JEWISH ENCYCLOPÆDIA describes the tract as devoted to speculations

concerning God and the angels—surely a very loose and incorrect account. Ginsburg, following Edersheim, HISTORY OF
THE JEWISH PEOPLE, terms it a monologue on the part of
Abraham, an inexact inference arising from the last paragraph,
to which I have alluded already as unauthentic in the opinion
of Mr Stenring, while it is regarded by Mordell as in perfect
harmony with all the original material. He affirms, however,
that it does not represent Abraham as author of the text itself,
but rather as inventor of the alphabet. It is an obscure
question, for the text itself is obscure, but it seems necessary
to recognise that there is a dual tradition in Kabalistic Jewry
according to which (1) Abraham wrote the SEPHER YETZIRAH,
the reason being given by A. Saadya, namely, to defend the
unity of God against the dualists and tritheists of Babylon ;
but alternatively (2) it was committed by God into the patriarch's
hands, as a bride is given to her husband.

Mr Stenring accepts the authorship of Rabbi Akiba as if it
were of common recognition in historical criticism or as if there
were actual evidence, and he has the authority of Professor
Schiller-Sznessy ; but it was challenged by Moses of Cordova in
the sixteenth century, and Mr Mordell does something to shew
that the attribution arose through a misconception. He is
disposed on his own part to refer the original portion to a
pre-Talmudic period and the additamenta to an undetermined
date between A.D. 750 and 931. The unknown author of a
commentary on the SEPHER preserved in the Bodleian and
referred to the thirteenth century ascribes it to Joseph ben
Uzziel by revelation of the prophet Jeremiah—meaning apparently that Joseph was the latter's disciple—or according to
another codex by communication from Joseph's grandfather
Ben Sira, he being the alleged grandson of Jeremiah and one of
the supposed authors of Ecclesiasticus. Hereof is some part
only of traditional ascriptions and at this it may be left, as
neither date nor authorship is likely to reach a settlement.
It remains that the text enforces the supreme unity of God
and His direct work in creation. Its chief " occult " aspect
is the implied virtue resident in Divine Names, with which
the deep and the height were sealed ; but this connotes for
myself a crude recognition of Divine Immanence in the universe.
From another point of view the conception belongs to conventional Magic of the so-called practical kind, and I have dealt
with the archæology of this subject in other writings. Its roots
are remote in the past and its last developments are in Grimoires

and Little Alberts. The occult student of modern times is not likely to attempt operations of a ceremonial kind with the aid of Tetragrammaton and its permutations, but Divine Names suggest numerical mysticism, which opens a wide field.

Mr Stenring institutes a comparison between the twenty-two letters of the Hebrew alphabet and the numerically corresponding symbols which constitute the Trumps Major of the Tarot cards. We owe this analogy to the ingenuity, such as it was, of Éliphas Lévi, who offered it for the acceptance of occultists in the RITUEL DE LA HAUTE MAGIE, 1856, claiming high authority and credit for the revelation of a great arcanum. As Mr Stenring offers us a new arrangement, which differs altogether from that of the French Magus, it is desirable to compare them for the benefit of those who are drawn to the old picture-symbols. The correspondences of Lévi are, however, arbitrary and recall his statements that the APOCALYPSE of St John and the TABLEAU NATUREL of Saint-Martin are based on the traditional sequence of the Trumps Major, his only evidence being that these widely divergent works are each divided into twenty-two chapters or sections—that of the first being of course an arrangement of early editors of the New Testament canon. Lévi's attribution was as follows : (1) *Aleph* = The Juggler, otherwise Magus ; (2) *Beth* = The Female Pope, or High Priestess ; (3) *Gimel* = The Empress ; (4) *Daleth* = The Emperor ; (5) *He* = The Pope, otherwise Hierophant ; (6) *Vau* = The Lovers ; (7) *Zayin* = The Chariot ; (8) *Cheth* = Justice ; (9) *Teth* = The Hermit, or Capuchin ; (10) *Yod* = The Wheel of Fortune ; (11) *Caph* = Strength ; (12) *Lamed* = The Hanged Man ; (13) *Mem* = Death ; (14) *Nun* = Temperance ; (15) *Samekh* = The Devil ; (16) *Ayin* = The Tower ; (17) *Pe* = The Star ; (18) *Tzaddi* = The Moon ; (19) *Quoph* = The Sun ; (20) *Resh* = The Last Judgment ; (21) *Shin* = The Fool ; (22) *Tau* = The World. Now, it is to be observed that the Fool = 0 in the Tarot sequence, but the letter *Shin* = 300 in the numerology of the Hebrew alphabet, so that in Lévi's arrangement the correspondence is to this extent voided.

The proper placing of the Tarot Fool is the great crux of every attempt—and there are several—to create a correspondence between the Trumps Major and the Hebrew letters. If it be worth while to say so, the correct sequence, which emerges from unexpected considerations, has never appeared in print, and it is not to be confused with a Victorian allocation now well known, but which used to be regarded as important :

it referred the cipher-card to *Aleph*, and therefore to the number one, so that we are confronted by the strange analogy of $0 = 1$, the alternative being—as we have seen—that $0 = 300$, otherwise 21 in the alphabetical order.

Mr Stenring's arrangement begins by referring the Tarot Minor Arcana to the Ten *Sephiroth* in the following order : (1) *Sephira* I = *Kether*, the Crown = The Four Aces ; (2) *Sephira* II = *Chokmah*, Wisdom = The Four Twos ;   ; (3) *Sephira* III = *Binah*, Understanding = The Four Threes ; (4) *Sephira* IV = *Chesed*, Mercy = The Four Fours ; (5) *Sephira* V = Geburah, Severity = The Four Fives ;   (6) *Sephira* VI = *Tiphereth*, Beauty = The Four Sixes ; (7) *Sephira* VII = *Netzach*, Victory = The Four Sevens ; (8) *Sephira* VIII = *Hod*, Glory = The Four Eights ; (9) *Sephira* IX = *Yesod*, Foundation = The Four Nines ; (10) *Sephira* X = *Malkuth*, The Kingdom = The Four Tens. It is to be observed that these allocations are derived from Lévi in his DOGME DE LA HAUTE MAGIE, 1854. See my translation, TRANSCENDENTAL MAGIC, etc., second edition, pp. 126, 127. The Trump cards of the Four Suits are referred by Mr Stenring to the Four Letters of Tetragrammaton : *Yod* = King in each suit ; *He* primal = Queen ; *Vau* = Knight ; and *He* final = Page, Knave or Jack. Lévi missed this obvious correspondence, referring the Four Letters generally to the suits themselves. I should mention that the names of the Sephiroth are found in the ZOHAR but not in the SEPHER YETZIRAH and not in the PATHS OF WISDOM.

So far as regards the Lesser Tarot Symbols and now in respect of the Trumps Major, Mr Stenring allocates as follows : (1) Three Mother Letters = *Aleph*, *Mem*, *Shin* = Juggler, World, Devil ; (2) Seven Double Letters = *Beth*, *Gimel*, *Daleth*, *Caph*, *Pe*, *Resh*, *Tau* = Sun, Moon, Chariot, Death, Hierophant, Star, Hanged Man ; (3) Twelve Simple Letters = *He*, *Vau*, *Zayin*, *Cheth*, *Teth*, *Yod*, *Lamed*, *Nun*, *Samekh*, *Ayin*, *Tzaddi*, *Quoph* = Empress, Emperor, High Priestess, Strength, Temperance, Lovers, Justice, Wheel of Fortune, Tower, Fool, Hermit, Judgment.

The natural sequence of Letters and Trumps Major works out therefore thus : (1) *Aleph* = Juggler ; (2) *Beth* = Sun ; (3) *Gimel* = Moon ; (4) *Daleth* = Chariot ; (5) *He* = Empress ; (6) *Vau* = Emperor ; (7) *Zayin* = High Priestess ; (8) *Cheth* = Strength ; (9) *Teth* = Temperance ; (10) *Yod* = Lovers ; (11) *Caph* = Death ; (12) *Lamed* = Justice ; (13) *Mem* = World ; (14) *Nun* = Wheel of Fortune ; (15) *Samekh* = Tower ;

(16) *Ayin* = Fool; (17) *Pe* = Pope or Hierophant; (18) *Tzaddi* = Hermit; (19) *Quoph* = Judgment; (20) *Resh* = Star; (21) *Shin* = Devil; (22) *Tau* = Hanged Man.

It will be seen that in this arrangement the Cipher Card is brought into correspondence with a Letter, the numerical value of which is 70 in Hebrew numeration. It should be noted further that in the PATHS OF WISDOM those which are numbered 11 to 32, both inclusive, have been referred by Kircher and others to their alphabetical correspondences according to the natural sequence of Letters; but in Mr Stenring's rearrangement—which deserves study—they are distributed according to the divisions of Mothers, Doubles and Simples, the titles of the Paths remaining unaltered, except in so far as Mr Stenring has transposed two of my own attributions made in the remote past and drawn at the time—if I remember rightly—from the classification adopted by a certain occult school. It should be understood that the attributions vary both in arrangement and titles in different codices. Those of Mr Stenring, Dr Westcott and myself may be compared with the enumeration of the Comtesse de Cimara on pp. 7, 8 of her French translation.

Mr Stenring claims (p. 26) that the Yetziratic meanings of Letters have enabled him to place the Tarot Trumps Major " in their original and proper order," referring no doubt to their redistribution in accordance with the triple division of the Hebrew alphabet. The correspondences of the Seven Doubles according to the SEPHER are Life, Peace, Wisdom, Wealth, Grace, Fruitfulness and Dominion, and according to Mr Stenring their Tarot correspondence are Sun, Moon, Chariot, Death, Hierophant, Star and Hanged Man. We may say that the Sun is Life, and astrologically we may connect the Moon with Peace, but I must leave to those who can discern them the analogies between Death and Wealth or the Hanged Man and Dominion. We get in fact the same kind of result throughout as would follow on a comparison of Tarot symbols with the traditional significations attached to the names of Hebrew letters as set forth in Table I. Accordingly, following Mr Stenring's arrangement, the Juggler answers to an Ox, the Moon-card to a Camel, the High Priestess to a Sword, Temperance to a Serpent, Death to the Palm of a Hand, the Hermit to a Fishing-Hook and the Devil to a Tooth. It may be well to add that I am not to be included among those who are satisfied that there is a valid correspondence between Hebrew letters and

Tarot Trump symbols. But Mr Stenring's arrangement seems to me wrought with exceeding care, and I have tabulated it therefore at length for the convenience of those who think otherwise.

As the GATES OF UNDERSTANDING are mentioned (p. 25), it may be said that they are exceedingly late, at least in their extant form, which is that of a treatise entitled GATES OF LIGHT, by R. Joseph Gikatilla ben Abraham (1248–1305 or later). I have explained elsewhere—DOCTRINE AND LITERATURE OF THE KABALAH, p. 78—that they begin with the First Matter, proceed through the putative elements to composite substances, thence to organic life, human nature, the heaven of the planets, that of the fixed stars, the *primum mobile*, the angelical orders, and finally to the archetypal world, unseen by mortal eye. There is no doubt that this is R. Joseph, developing Zoharic intimations into a conventional system. For the ZOHAR has references to the Fifty Gates, but they convey very different impressions. Those who are curious concerning them may consult my SECRET DOCTRINE IN ISRAEL, p. 251, where they are collected together. According to the great storehouse of rabbinical theosophy, (1) those who study the Law open the GATES OF BINAH ; (2) they are Gates of Salvation ; (3) they are in the region of the Supreme Mother, otherwise that Shekinah in Transcendence who gives power to the Mother below, and she is the Shekinah in manifestation ; (4) they are also Gates of Compassion, and the last of all, leading from *Binah* to *Chokmah*, or from Supernal Understanding to Supernal Wisdom, was not opened by Moses, because he was in separation from his wife. To realise all that is implied by the last statement, for the fact of which there is authority in the TALMUD, it must be understood that the high intent of the ZOHAR is fixed upon what is called the Mystery of Faith, and this is a Mystery of Sex. In the last resource it is the Mystery of Union between Jehovah and Elohim, or God and His Shekinah, represented by JOD, HE in the Divine Name. Mr Stenring points out that the number 50 is written in Hebrew with the letters KL = All, and he remembers no doubt the allusions to this word in the GATES OF LIGHT. But in the ZOHAR, because of the Mystery of Union, the number of the Gates is obtained by the multiplication of Yod = 10 and He = 5 = 50. It follows that in Zoharic understanding the Gates are Gates of Union, and those who study the Law shall pass thereby into the term thereof.

A. E. WAITE.

# TRANSLATOR'S NOTE

THE "Book of Formation" embodies the fundamental part of the secret learning, or Kabala, of the Jews. This tradition (Kabala means "to hand down") was probably never put into writing until Rabbi Akiba ben Joseph produced the "Book of Formation," or "Book of Numbers and Letters," in the second century after Christ. In order to render his work unintelligible for the profane he used a veiled language, and expressed himself in riddles and conundrums. Owing to this mysterious language the book has been misunderstood, and the philosophical and magical system of the Kabala classified as unreasonable.

The present version of "Sepher Yetzirah" is a word-for-word translation from the Hebrew, and a list of the texts used for this purpose will be found on the last page. Those portions of the text which we regard as genuine are printed in ordinary type, and the spurious passages in italics. Words placed within brackets are additions or renderings made by us.

The student is advised to make himself acquainted with the genuine verses of "Sepher Yetzirah" and the illustrative notes thereon before he proceeds to "The 32 Paths of Wisdom."

It is hoped that the elucidations provided in the notes will not only reawaken interest in the text itself but in Kabalistic philosophy at large and lead to a much-needed renaissance of occultism.

KNUT STENRING.

HELSINGBORG, SWEDEN, 1923.

TABLE I.—HEBREW AND CHALDEE LETTERS

| Number. | Power. | Hebrew and Chaldee letters. | Numerical value. | Expressed in this work by: | Name. | Signification of name. |
|---|---|---|---|---|---|---|
| 1 | Mother | א | 1 | A | Aleph | Ox. |
| 2 | Double | ב | 2 | B | Beth | House. |
| 8 | Double | ג | 8 | G | Gimel | Camel. |
| 4 | Double | ד | 4 | D | Daleth | Door. |
| 5 | Simple | ה | 5 | H | He | Window. |
| 6 | Simple | ו | 6 | V | Vau | Peg, nail. |
| 7 | Simple | ז | 7 | Z | Zayin | Weapon, sword. |
| 8 | Simple | ח | 8 | Ch | Cheth | Enclosure, fence. |
| 9 | Simple | ט | 9 | T | Teth | Serpent. |
| 10 | Simple | י | 10 | I | Yod | Hand. |
| 11 | Double | כ  Final—ך | 20  Final—500 | K } Kf | Caph | Palm of the hand. |
| 12 | Simple | ל | 30 | L | Lamed | Ox-goad. |
| 18 | Mother | מ  Final—ם | 40  Final—600 | M } Mf | Mem | Water. |
| 14 | Simple | נ  Final—ן | 50  Final—700 | N } Nf | Nun | Fish. |
| 15 | Simple | ס | 60 | S | Samekh | Prop, support. |
| 16 | Simple | ע | 70 | O | Ayin | Eye. |
| 17 | Double | פ  Final—ף | 80  Final—800 | P } Pf | Pe | Mouth. |
| 18 | Simple | צ  Final—ץ | 90  Final—900 | Tz } Tzf | Tzaddi | Fishing-hook. |
| 19 | Simple | ק | 100 | Q | Qoph | Back of the head. |
| 20 | Double | ר | 200 | R | Resh | Head. |
| 21 | Mother | ש | 800 | Sh | Shin | Tooth. |
| 22 | Double | ת | 400 | Th | Tau | Sign of the cross. |

*With the exception of the second column, this table is according to S. L. MacGregor Mathers.*

# CHAPTER I

1. IN thirty-two mysterious paths of wisdom did the Lord write, *the Lord of Hosts, the God of Israel, the Living Elohim, and King of the Universe, the Almighty, Merciful, and Gracious God; He is great and exalted and eternally dwelling in the Height, His name is holy, He is exalted and holy.* He created His Universe by the three forms of expression : Numbers, Letters, and Words.

2. Ten ineffable Sephiroth and twenty-two basal letters : three mothers, seven double, and twelve simple (letters).

3. Ten ineffable Sephiroth, corresponding to the ten fingers, five (over) against five and the only token of the covenant in the middle : the word of the tongue and (the circumcision) of the flesh.

4. Ten ineffable Sephiroth, ten and not nine, ten and not eleven : understand with wisdom and apprehend with care ; examine by means of them and search them out ; *know, count, and write.* Put forth the subject in its light and place the Formator on His throne. He is the only Creator and the only Formator, and no one exists but He : His attributes are ten and have no limits.

5. The ineffable Sephiroth : their totality is ten ; they are, however, without limits : the infinity of the Beginning and the infinity of the End, the infinity of the Good and the infinity of the Evil, the infinity of the Height and the infinity of the Depth, the infinity of the East and the infinity of the West, the infinity of (the) North and the infinity of (the) South ; *and only one Lord God, the trusty King, rules them all from His holy dwelling in all eternity.*

6. Ten ineffable Sephiroth : their appearance is like that of a flash of lightning, their goal is infinite. His word is in them when they emanate and when they return ; at His bidding do they haste like a whirlwind ; and before His throne do they prostrate (themselves).

7. Ten ineffable Sephiroth : their end is in their beginning and likewise their beginning in their end, as the flame is bound to the burning coal. *Know, count, and write.* The Lord is one and the Formator is one and hath no second (beside Him) : what number canst thou count before one ?

8. Ten ineffable Sephiroth : close thy mouth lest it speak and thy heart lest it think ; and if thy mouth openeth for utterance and thy heart turneth toward thought, bring them back (to thy control). LMQVMf, *therefore it is written :* " *And the living creatures ran and returned* " (Ezekiel i. 14) ; and hence was the covenant made.

9. Ten ineffable Sephiroth :

One—The Spirit of the Living Elohim, His throne is erected in eternity, *blessed and praised be His name, the Living God of ages, eternal and forever ; Voice, Spirit, and Word : this is the Spirit of the Holy One. His beginning hath no beginning and His end hath no ending.*

10. Two—Air from Spirit : He wrote and formed therein twenty-two basal letters ; three mothers, seven double, and twelve simple.

11. Three—Water from Air : He wrote and formed therein twenty-two letters, from the formless and void—mire and clay ; He designed them as a platband, He hewed them as a wall, He covered them as a building, He poured snow over them and it became earth, *even as it is written :* " *He saith to the snow : Be thou the earth* " (Job xxxvii. 6).

12. Four—Fire from Water : and He designed and cut thereof the Throne of Glory : Seraphim, Ophanim, the Holy Animals, the Ministering Angels ; and with these three He founded His dwelling. *Therefore it is written :* " *He maketh His angels spirits and His ministers a flaming fire* " (Ps. civ. 4).

18. He chose three of the simple letters, a secret belonging to the three mothers, אמש = A M Sh, and put them in His Great Name and sealed with them six extensions.

Five—He sealed the Height stretched upwards and sealed it with יהו = IHV.

Six—He sealed the Depth stretched downwards and sealed it with יוה = IVH.

Seven—He sealed the East stretched forwards and sealed it with היו = HIV.

Eight—He sealed the West stretched backwards and sealed it with הוי = HVI.

Nine—He sealed the (North) stretched to the right and sealed it with ויה = VIH.

Ten—He sealed the (South) stretched to the left and sealed it with והי = VHI.

14. *These are the ten ineffable Sephiroth : one—the Spirit of the Living Elohim ; two—Air from Spirit ; three—Water from Air ; four—Fire from Water ; Height, Depth, East, West, North, and South.*

# CHAPTER II

1. TWENTY-TWO basal letters : three mothers, seven double, and twelve simple. *Three mothers :* אמש = *A M Sh, their foundation : the scale of Merit and the scale of Guilt, and the tongue is (an) equilibrating law between the two. Three mothers : A M Sh—M is mute, Sh is sibilant, and A equilibrates the two.*

2. Twenty-two basal letters : He designed them, He formed them, He purified them, He weighed them, and He exchanged them, each one with all ; He formed by means of them the whole creation and everything that should be created (subsequently).

3. *Twenty-two basal letters : three mothers, seven double, and twelve simple ; they are designed in the voice, formed in the air and set in the mouth at five places.*

| The letters : | | |
|---|---|---|
| אהחע = *A H Ch O* | *at the throat,* | |
| גיכק = *G I K Q* | *at the palate,* | |
| בטלנת = *B T L N Th* | *at the tongue,* | |
| זסצרש = *Z S Tz R Sh* | *at the teeth,* | |
| דומפ = *D V M P* | *at the lips.* | |

4. Twenty-two basal letters : they are placed together in a ring, as a wall with two hundred and thirty-one gates. The ring may be put in rotation forwards or backwards and its token is this : Nothing excels ענג = ONG ( =pleasure) in good, and nothing excels נגע = NGO ( =plague) in evil.

5. How did He combine, weigh, and exchange them ? A with all and all with A ; B with all and all with B ; G with all and all with G ; and all of them turned round. Hence they go forth through two hundred and thirty-one gates, and thus it comes about that the whole creation and all language proceed from one combination of letters.

6. He created from the formless and made the non-existent exist ; and He formed large columns out of intangible air. This is the token : He beheld, exchanged, and brought forth the whole creation and all objects (by means of) one combination of letters, the token of which is twenty-two objects in one body.

# CHAPTER III

1. THREE mothers : אמש = A M Sh. Their foundation is : the scale of Merit and the scale of Guilt, and the tongue is (an) equilibrating law between the two.

2. Three mothers : A M Sh. This is a great, recondite, hidden, and precious secret, sealed with six seals, and from these (A M Sh) proceeded Air, Water, and Fire. *Fathers were produced by them, and from the fathers (descend) the generations.*

3. Three mothers : A M Sh. He designed, formed, purified, weighed, and exchanged them; and by means of them He brought forth three mothers in the Universe, three mothers in the Year, three mothers in Man, *male and female.*

4. *Three mothers : A M Sh—Fire, Air, and Water. The heavens are produced from Fire, the wind is produced from Air, and the earth is produced from Water : the Fire above and the Water below, and the Air is (an) equilibrating law between the two ; by them were the fathers brought forth, and by them were all things produced.*

5. Three mothers : A M Sh in the Universe—Air, Water, and Fire. The heavens were in the beginning produced from Fire, the earth from Water, and the wind from Air, which thus equilibrates the two.

6. Three mothers : A M Sh in the Year—the cold, the heat, and the temperate state. The heat was produced from Fire, the cold from Water, and the temperate state from Air, which thus equilibrates the two.

7. Three mothers : A M Sh in Man—the head, the belly, and the chest. The head was produced from Fire, the belly from Water, and the chest from Air, which thus equilibrates the two.

8. He caused the letter A to reign in Air, bound a crown upon it and fused them together. He produced by means of them : the atmosphere in the Universe, the temperate state in the Year, and the chest in Man, *male and female.*

9. He caused the letter M to reign in Water, bound a crown upon it and fused them together. He produced by means of

them the earth in the Universe, the cold in the Year, and the belly in Man, *male and female.*

10. He caused the letter Sh to reign in Fire, bound a crown upon it and fused them together. He produced by means of them the heavens in the Universe, the heat in the Year, and the head in Man, *male and female.*

# CHAPTER IV

1. SEVEN double (letters) : בגדכפרת = B G D K P R Th. Their foundation is : Life, Peace, Wisdom, Wealth, Beauty, Fruitfulness, and Dominion.

2. Seven double : B G D K P R Th. They are pronounced in two ways : B B, G G, D D, K K, P P, R R, Th Th : according to the form of the soft and hard, the strong and weak breathing.

3. Seven double : B G D K P R Th, according to pronunciation and permutation : contrary to Life is Death, contrary to Peace is Misfortune, contrary to Wisdom is Folly, contrary to Wealth is Poverty, contrary to Beauty is Ugliness, contrary to Fruitfulness is Devastation, contrary to Dominion is Slavery.

4. Seven double : B G D K P R Th, Height, Depth, East, West, North, and South, and the Holy Palace in the middle, which sustains them all.

5. *Seven double : B G D K P R Th, seven and not six, seven and not eight; examine and search out by means of them, bring the subject forth into light and place the Formator on His throne.*

6. Seven double : B G D K P Th. He designed, formed, purified, weighed, and exchanged them; He produced by means of them seven planets in the Universe, seven days in the Year, and seven gateways in Man; *and by means of them also He designed seven heavens, seven earths, and seven weeks. Therefore of all things under the heavens did He love the heptad.*

7. These are the seven planets in the Universe : Saturn, Jupiter, Mars, Sun, Venus, Mercury, Moon. These are the seven days in the Year; the seven days of the week; seven gateways in Man—two eyes, two ears, two nostrils, and the mouth.

8. He caused the letter B to reign in Wisdom, bound a crown upon it and fused them together. He produced by means of them : (the Sun) in the Universe, Sunday in the Year, and the right eye in Man, *male and female.*

9. He caused the letter G to reign in Wealth, bound a crown upon it and fused them together; He produced by means of them : (the Moon) in the Universe, Monday in the Year, and the left eye in Man, *male and female.*

83

10. He caused the letter D to reign in Fruitfulness, bound a crown upon it and fused them together. He produced by means of them : (Mars) in the Universe, Tuesday in the Year, and the right ear in Man, *male and female.*

11. He caused the letter K to reign in Life, bound a crown upon it and fused them together. He produced by means of them : (Mercury) in the Universe, Wednesday in the year, and the left ear in Man, *male and female.*

12. He caused the letter P to reign in Dominion, bound a crown upon it and fused them together. He produced by means of them : (Jupiter) in the Universe, Thursday in the Year, and the right nostril in Man, *male and female.*

13. He caused the letter R to reign in Peace, bound a crown upon it and fused them together. He produced by means of them : (Venus) in the Universe, Friday in the Year, and the left nostril in Man, *male and female.*

14. He caused the letter Th to reign in Beauty, bound a crown upon it and fused them together. He produced by means of them : (Saturn) in the Universe, Saturday in the Year, and the mouth in Man, *male and female.*

15. *Seven double : B G D K P R Th. There were designed by means of them, seven earths, seven heavens, seven continents, seven seas, seven rivers, seven deserts, seven days, seven weeks, seven years, seven fallow-years, seven jubilees, and the Holy Palace : hence under all the heavens did He love the heptad.*

16. Seven double : B G D K P R Th. How did He fuse them together ? Two stones build two houses, three stones build six houses, four stones build twenty-four houses, five stones build one hundred and twenty houses, six stones build seven hundred and twenty houses, seven stones build five thousand and forty houses. Make a beginning herefrom and calculate further what the mouth cannot pronounce and what the ear cannot hear.

# CHAPTER V

1. TWELVE simple (letters) : הוזחטילנסעצק = H V Z Ch T I L N S O Tz Q. Their foundation is : Sight, Hearing, Smell, Speech, Taste, Coition, Work, Movement, Wrath, Mirth, Meditation, Sleep.

2. Twelve simple : H V Z Ch T I L N S O Tz Q, twelve and not eleven, twelve and not thirteen. Their foundation corresponds to the twelve oblique angles (or directions) : the North-East angle, the South-East angle, the above-East angle, the below-East angle, the above-North angle, the below-North angle, the North-West angle, the South-West angle, the above-West angle, the below-West angle, the above-South angle, the below-South angle. And they stretch out and diverge into infinity : *these are the arms of Universe.*

3. Twelve simple : H V Z Ch T I L N S O Tz Q. He designed, formed, purified, exchanged, and weighed them, and produced by means of them twelve zodiacal signs in the Universe, twelve months in the Year, and twelve chief (members) in Man, *male and female.*

4. Twelve zodiacal signs in the Universe : Aries, Taurus, Gemini, Cancer, Leo, Virgo, Libra, Scorpio, Sagittarius, Capricornus, Aquarius, Pisces.

5. Twelve months in the Year : Nisan, Ijar, Sivan, Tamuz, Abh, Elul, Tišri, Marḥešvan, Kislev, Ṭebeth, Šebath, Adār.

6. Twelve chief (members) in Man, *male and female* : two hands, two feet, two kidneys, the liver, the spleen, the gall, the stomach, the colon, the bowels. *He made them according to the order of a battle, even one against the other made God.*

7. He caused the letter H to reign in Sight, bound a crown upon it and fused them together ; He produced by means of them : Aries in the Universe, Nisan in the Year, and the right hand in man, *male and female.*

8. He caused the letter V to reign in Hearing, bound a crown upon it and fused them together ; He produced by means of them : Taurus in the Universe, Ijar in the Year, and the left hand in Man, *male and female.*

9. He caused the letter Z to reign in Smell, bound a crown upon it and fused them together; He produced by means of them : Gemini in the Universe, Sivan in the Year, and the right foot in Man, *male and female.*

10. He caused the letter Ch to reign in Speech, bound a crown upon it and fused them together; He produced by means of them : Cancer in the Universe, Tamuz in the Year, and the left foot in Man, *male and female.*

11. He caused the letter T to reign in Taste, bound a crown upon it and fused them together; He produced by means of them : Leo in the Universe, Abh in the Year, and the right kidney in Man, *male and female.*

12. He caused the letter I to reign in Coition, bound a crown upon it and fused them together; He produced by means of them : Virgo in the Universe, Elul in the Year, and the left kidney in Man, *male and female.*

13. He caused the letter L to reign in Work, bound a crown upon it and fused them together; He produced by means of them : Libra in the Universe, Tišri in the Year, and the liver in Man, *male and female.*

14. He caused the letter N to reign in Movement, bound a crown upon it and fused them together; He produced by means of them : Scorpio in the Universe, Marhešvan in the Year, and the spleen in Man, *male and female.*

15. He caused the letter S to reign in Wrath, bound a crown upon it and fused them together; He produced by means of them : Sagittarius in the Universe, Kislev in the Year, and the gall in Man, *male and female.*

16. He caused the letter O to reign in Mirth, bound a crown upon it and fused them together; He produced by means of them : Capricornus in the Universe, Tebeth in the Year, and the stomach in Man, *male and female.*

17. He caused the letter Tz to reign in Meditation, bound a crown upon it and fused them together; He produced by means of them : Aquarius in the Universe, Šebath in the Year, and the colon in Man, *male and female.*

18. He caused the letter Q to reign in Sleep, bound a crown upon it and fused them together; He produced by means of them : Pisces in the Universe, Adār in the Year, and the bowels in Man, *male and female.*

19. He made them according to the art of warfare, arranged them as a wall, and armed them as for battle.

# CHAPTER VI

1. THERE are three mothers, *that are three fathers*; from them proceed Fire, Air, and Water. Three mothers, seven double, and twelve simple.

2. (A M Sh, B G D K P R Th, H V Z Ch T I L N S O Tz Q). These are the twenty-two letters by means of which the Holy (One), *blessed be He, the Lord, the Lord of Hosts, the Living Elohim, the God of Israel,* hath founded (everything). *He is great and exalted, the One Who dwelleth (in the Height) eternally. His name is exalted and holy; He is exalted and holy.*

3. A proof of this and true tokens are: the Universe, the Year, and Man. Twelve are beneath, seven upon these, and three upon the seven. From the three He founded His dwelling and everything proceeds from one. This is a token that He is One and hath no second (beside Him). He is the only King in the Universe, He is one and His name is One.

4. The numbers of the Universe are ten (and twelve); a proof of this and true tokens are: *the Universe, the Year, and Man*; Fire, Air, and Water, seven planets and twelve zodiacal signs.

The numbers of the Year are ten (and twelve): cold, heat, and the temperate state, seven days and twelve months.

The numbers of Man are ten and twelve: head, belly, and breast, seven gateways and twelve chief members.

5. *These are the three mothers: A M Sh; from these proceeded fathers, and from the fathers (descend) generations. Three fathers and their generations, seven planets and their hosts, and twelve oblique angles. A proof of this and true tokens are: the Universe, the Year, and Man.*

6. A law is: the dodecad, the heptad, and the triad; their commissioners are: the dragon, the (celestial) sphere, and the heart.

7. *Three mothers, A M Sh—Air, Water, and Fire; Fire above, Water below, and the Air is an equilibrating law between the two. The token is: the Fire carries the Water; M is mute, Sh is sibilant, and A is an equilibrating law between the two.*

8. The dragon in the Universe is like a king on his throne; the (celestial) sphere in the Year is like a king in a province; the heart (in Man) is like a king in warfare.

9. God hath also set one thing against the other; the good against the evil and the evil against the good, good from good and evil from evil; the good marks out the evil and the evil marks out the good; good is reserved for the good ones and evil is reserved for the evil ones.

10. Three: each one stands alone for himself; one merited, one loaded with guilt, and one equilibrating between the two.

11. Seven are divided, three against three and one is equilibrating between the two groups.

12. Twelve are in warfare, *three friends and three enemies, three life-givers, three destroyers.*

13. *Three friends: the heart and the ears; three enemies: the gall, the tongue, and the liver; three life-givers: the two nostrils and the spleen; three destroyers: the two (lower) apertures and the mouth; and God, a trusty King, ruleth them all from His holy place in all eternity.*

14. One over three, three over seven, seven over twelve, and all are joined one to the other, a token of which is twenty-two objects in one body.

15.             (A M Sh
            B G D K P R Th
        H V Z Ch T I L N S O Tz Q.)

These are the twenty-two letters by means of which אהיה = AHIH, יה = IH, יהוה = IHVH, אלהים = ALHIM, אלהים יהוה = ALHIM IHVH, יהוה צבאות = IHVH TzBAVTh, אלהים צבאות = ALHIM TzBAVTh, אל = AL, שדי = ShDI, יהוה אדני = IHVH ADNI, hath designed (all); He made three numbers of them and formed His whole world of them; by means of them He formed the whole creation and all that shall yet be created.

16. *And when our father Abraham, peace be with him, had come, he beheld, contemplated, studied, and understood this; he formed and designed till he had reached it, then the Lord of the Universe, blessed be His name, appeared to him. He took him to His bosom and kissed him on his head and called him Abraham His friend; He made a covenant with him and his children, therefore it is written: " He had faith in the Lord." This was ascribed to him justly. He (the Lord) put the token of the covenant between his (Abraham's) hands, that is, the tongue; and between the feet, that is, the circumcision. He bound the twenty-two letters of the Thora to his tongue, and the Holy One, blessed be He, unveiled to him His secret. He let them (the letters) soak in Water, burn in Fire, and sway in the Air; He let them shine in the seven stars and lead in the twelve zodiacal signs.*

TABLE II.—THE 10 SEPHIROTH ACCORDING TO "SEPHER YETZIRAH."

| 1. | 2. | 3. | 4. | 5. | 6. | 7. | 8. | 9. | 10. |
|---|---|---|---|---|---|---|---|---|---|
| Infinity of Beginning. | Infinity of End. | Infinity of Good. | Infinity of Evil. | Infinity of Height. | Infinity of Depth. | Infinity of East. | Infinity of West. | Infinity of North. | Infinity of South. |
| Transcendental SPIRIT. | Transcendental Air. | Transcendental Water. | Transcendental Fire. | Transcendental Height. | Transcendental Depth. | Transcendental East. | Transcendental West. | Transcendental North. | Transcendental South. |
| | 22 Foundation-letters. | Transcendental Matter. (The essence of Od.) | Transcendental Life. (The essence of Vitality.) | IHV. | IVH. | HIV. | HVI. | VIH. | VHI. |

TABLE III.—THE 3 MOTHERS ACCORDING TO "SEPHER YETZIRAH."

| | M. The essence of Water. | A. The essence of Air. | Sh. The essence of Fire. |
|---|---|---|---|
| Their Foundation : | Merit. (mute) (Guilt.) | The equilibrating power. | Guilt. (sibilant) (Merit.) |
| Universe (M) : | Earth. | Atmosphere. | Heavens. |
| The Year (A) : | Cold. | Temperate state. | Heat. |
| Man (Sh) : | Belly. | Chest. | Head. |

Equilibrated forces. Perfect harmony.

TABLE IV.—THE 7 DOUBLES ACCORDING TO "SEPHER YETZIRAH."

| ✡ | B. | G. | D. | K. | P. | R. | Th. |
|---|---|---|---|---|---|---|---|
| Their correspondence in space: | Height. | Depth. | East. | West. | North. | South. | The Holy Palace in the middle. |
| Their foundation: | Wisdom. Folly. | Wealth. Poverty. | Fruitfulness. Devastation. | Life. Death. | Dominion. Slavery. | Peace. Misfortune. | Beauty. Ugliness. |
| Universe (M): | Sun. | Moon. | Mars. | Mercury. | Jupiter. | Venus. | Saturn. |
| The Year. (A): | Sunday. | Monday. | Tuesday. | Wednesday. | Thursday. | Friday. | Saturday. |
| Man. (Sh): | Right Eye. | Left Eye. | Right Ear. | Left Ear. | Right Nostril. | Left Nostril. | Mouth. |

Changeable forces.

TABLE V.—THE 12 SIMPLES ACCORDING TO "SEPHER YETZIRAH."

| | H. | V. | Z. | Ch. | T. | L. | L. | N. | S. | O. | Tz. | Q. |
|---|---|---|---|---|---|---|---|---|---|---|---|---|
| Their correspondence in space : | North-East. | South-East. | Height-East. | Depth-East. | Height-North. | Depth-North. | North-West. | South-West. | Height-West. | Depth-West. | Height-South. | Depth-South. |
| Their Foundation : | Sight. | Hearing. | Smell. | Speech. | Eating. | Coition. | Work. | Movement. | Wrath. | Mirth. | Meditation. | Sleep. |
| Universe (M) : | Aries. | Taurus. | Gemini. | Cancer. | Leo. | Virgo. | Libra. | Scorpio. | Sagittarius. | Capricornus. | Aquarius. | Pisces. |
| The Year (A) : | *Mar. 21–Apr. 19.* Nisan. | *Apr. 19–May 20.* Ijar. | *May 20–June 21* Sivan. | *June 21–July 22* Tamuz. | *July 22–Aug. 22.* Abh. | *Aug. 22–Sept. 23.* Elul. | *Sept. 23–Oct. 23.* Tišri. | *Oct. 23–Nov. 22.* Marḥešvan. | *Nov. 22–Dec. 21* Kislev. | *Dec. 21–Jan. 20.* Tebeth. | *Jan. 20–Feb. 19.* Šebath. | *Feb. 19–Mar. 21.* Adār. |
| Man (Sh) : | Right Hand. | Left Hand. | Right Foot. | Left Foot. | Right Kidney. | Left Kidney. | Liver. | Milt. | Gall. | Stomach. | Rennet-bag. | Bowels. |

Constant forces. Strife.

# NOTES

**The Book of Formation.**—ספר יצירה = SPR ITzIRH (" Sepher Yetzirah ").

**Book.**—SPR =book, letter.

**Formation.**—ITzIRH =formation, creation (Gen. ii. 7).

After setting aside provisionally those portions of " Sepher Yetzirah " which, on account of their content, we have come to regard as spurious, it was found that 72 verses remained, and may be taken to constitute the original text, as written by Rabbi Akiba. The old mystics sought to harmonise the outer form of a book with its inward significance, and the number 72 is in perfect correspondence with the subject-matter of " Sepher Yetzirah," because it can be derived from the name of the Lord in the following manner: IHVH, IHV, IH, I $(10+5+6+5)+(10+5+6)$ $+(10+5)+10=72$. (Comp. the Schemahamphorasch, Exod. xiv. 19, 20, 21.)

## CHAPTER I

The main subject in this chapter is The Ten Sephiroth, the transcendental nature of which may be termed obvious. See Table II.

I. 1. **32 paths of wisdom.**—לב נתיבות פליאות = LB NThIBVTh PLIAVTh.

**wisdom.**—PLIAVTh =mystical wisdom.

In the Biblical narrative of the creation (Gen. i.) the name of Elohim is mentioned 32 times. 32 =LB in Hebrew characters, and signifies " Heart," a symbol of spirituality and intelligence.

*Considering the Mind of man as a faint reflex of the Universal Mind, which is God, it follows that any human idea is the vague image of a perfect idea, which is of God. Man endeavours to idealise this dim mind-picture, and the result is a symbol which, so far as human intelligence can reach, will be in the likeness of the perfect idea. Man cannot think without the use of symbols.*

The 32 Paths of Wisdom are 32 notions which comprehend the whole creation. Under these fundamental ideas all that exists is classified. When the Lord wrote a " Number " or a " Letter," in each of these paths forces were created " from " which everything was formed. By means of their symbols — otherwise " Numbers " and " Letters "—these forces became apprehensible for the human Mind. Thus, by means of their numbers and names (their symbols) they can be communicated " to holy men, after long toil, long experience of divine things, and long meditation thereon." To reach an absolute knowledge of only one of these mystical paths of divine wisdom is, however, impossible for the human mind. He who endeavours to climb to these supreme heights of wisdom must first pass through " The 50 Gates of Understanding." In other words, He must acquire an encyclopædic knowledge of all sciences. 50, in Hebrew characters KL, means " All." (כלה = K L H =the bride of Microprosopus. K NST L, Ecclesia Israel, Zion, the Holy Palace. See Notes IV. 4.)

I. i. the Lord.—יה = IH =Kurios (Gr.), Dominus (Lat.). (Ps. lxviii. 4.)

This name is the first half of Tetragrammaton, יהוה = IHVH, the name that must not be pronounced.

The Lord of hosts.—יהוה צבאות = IHVH TzBAVTh (Ps. xxiv. 10).

The God (of Israel).—אלהים = ALHIM =the " strong " God (of Israel).

The Living Elohim.—אלהים חיים = ALHIMf ChIIMf = the Living Elohim, the Elohim of Life.

ALHIMf is a plural form, and is by some Kabalists supposed to be the seven forces that emanated from the only God in order to control the manifested world, " Terra viventium " (?). By others it is thought to be an expression for the Trinity of God as found in late Christianity (?).

God.—אל = AL =God, strong.

Numbers, Letters, and Words.—בספר וספר וספור = BSPR VSPR (or VSVPR) VSPVR.

These words are undoubtedly derived from the same root, viz. ספר = SPR =book, letter, numbering, word, sound (2 Chron. ii. 17).

| Pistorius | gives : | scriptis, numeratis, pronunciatis. |
| Postellus | ,, | numerans, numerus, numeratus. |
| Rittangelius | ,, | numero, numerante, numerato. |
| Goldschmidt | ,, | Zahl, Zähler, Gezähltes. |
| Cimara | ,, | l'Ecriture, le Nombre, la Parole. |
| Westcott | ,, | Numbers, Letters, Sounds. |
| Stenring | ,, | Numbers, Letters, Words. |

Numbers signify transcendental forces, *i.e.*, the ten Sephiroth. Letters signify basal forces, and these are twenty-two. Words signify the combination of forces, *i.e.*, the two hundred and thirty-one gates (" S. Y.," Chapter II. 4 and 5). These three forms of expression are the symbols of " Prima Faktora."

I. 2. **Sephiroth.**—ספירות = SPIRVTh =number.
 =it can be a deriva-
 tion from σφαῖρα
 (Gr.), Sphere.
 =predicationes logicæ
 (Buxtorf).
 =spiritus (Lat.) (West-
 cott).

**ineffable Sephiroth.**—(עשר = OShR) ספירות בלימה = SPIRVTh BLIMH (Job xxvi. 7).

| Pistorius | gives : | præter ineffabile. |
| Postellus | ,, | belimah Sephiroth. |
| Rittangelius | ,, | præter illud ineffabile. |
| Goldschmidt | ,, | Zahlen ohne etwas. |
| Cimara | ,, | Séphiroths ineffables. |
| Westcott | ,, | ineffable Sephiroth. |

**Twenty-two basal letters** are twenty-two creating ideas or forces which human intelligence has symbolised in the " Book of Thoth," or the major trump cards of Tarot. The Hebrew letters which in Kabalism are used as symbols of these 32 creating ideas are, in fact, the trump cards of Tarot. The meaning which " Sepher Yetzirah " assigns to each letter has enabled us to place the Tarot-cards in their original and proper order, being that of the Paths of Wisdom.

I. 3. The literal translation of the last part of this verse is as follows : " and the only token in the middle—מילה = MILH—of the tongue and of membrum virile." MILH =(has a double meaning) word, circumcision.

The covenant that God made with Abraham (Gen. xvii.) had one spiritual and one material aspect. The token of the covenant had also one spiritual and one material aspect. The spiritual aspect of the token was the word of the tongue : " Neither shall thy name any more be ABRM, but thy name shall be ABRHM." This was the sign of God to make a great people of Abraham and his seed. The material aspect of the token was the circumcision of the flesh : " And ye shall circumcise the flesh of your foreskin." This was the sign of Abraham's and his seed's obedience to God and His commandments.

**I. 4. throne,** place.

**I. 5. infinity.**—OVMQ, or (OMQ) =infinity, profoundness.

**Good.**—עגב = ONG =good, pleasure.
**Evil.**—נגע = NGO =evil, plague. } (" S. Y.," II. 4.)

**Height.**—רום = RVMf.

**Depth.**—עמק = OMQ, or (OVMQ). (MTH.)

**East.**—מזרח = MZRCh.

**West.**—מערב = MORB.

**North.**—צפון = TzPVNf.

**South.**—דרום = DRVMf.

**Lord.**—יהיד = IHID. $10+5+10+4=29$. $2+9=11=10+1$. *The Sephirotic forces plus the force of Union. Ten in one (Fig. 1).*

**God.**—אל = AL. (Notes I. 1.)

**I. 6. flash of lightning.**—The ten Sephiroth are often tabulated along a zigzag line.

**emanate.**—go out. On this verse rests the Sephirotic emanation theory which is further developed in Zohar.

**I. 7. Their end is in their beginning and likewise their beginning in their end.**—This signifies the transcendental nature of the 10 Sephiroth (Fig. 1).

**the Lord.**—יהיד = IHID. (Notes I. 5.)

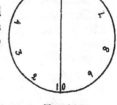

Fɪɢ 1.

**I. 8.** Rabbi Akiba utters a warning against vain talk about the 10 ineffable Sephiroth and loose speculations on their nature, but, at the same time, he points out that the covenant was made by means of self-control and concentration of thought. This verse forms an introduction to the following five verses :—

LMQVMf.—? (מקום = MQVMf = place, location, spot.)

**I. 9. Spirit.**—רוח = RVCh =spirit, air.
**the Living Elohim.** (Notes I. 1.)
**in,** from, since.
**God.**—אל = AL. (Notes I. 1.)
**Voice.**—קול = QVL.
**Word.**—דבר = DBR, or VDBVR.

**I. 10. Air from Spirit.**—The Breath of the Spirit of God. Transcendental Air.

**Air.**—רוח = RVCh.

**I. 11. Water from Air.**—The moisture of the Breath of the Spirit of God. Transcendental Water. The essence of the Od.

**Water.**—מים = MIMf.

**wrote,** designed.

**formless.**—תהו = ThHV.

**void.**—בהו = BHV (Gen. i. 2; Isa. xxxiv. 11).

(According to Cimara, Tohu is negative and can be formed by Bohu, which is positive.)

**snow.**—שלג = ShLG.

**earth.**—עפר = OPR.

The creation of transcendental matter and transcendental form. Order.

**I. 12. Fire from Water.**—The warmth or fire contained within the moisture breathed forth by the Spirit of God. Transcendental Fire. The essence of Vitality (Gen. ii. 7).

**Fire.**—אש = ASh.

**Throne of Glory.**—כסא הכבוד = KSA HKBVD.

**Seraphim.**—שרפים = ShRPIMf =(Fiery) Serpents (Isa. vi. 2; Num. xxi. 6, 8).·

**Ophanim.**—אופנים = AVPNIMf =Wheel (Ezek. i. 16).

**Holy Animals.**—חיות הקדש = ChIVTh HQDSh, or (HQVDSh) =Holy Animals, Living Creatures, Cherubim (Gen. iii. 24; Exod. xxv. 18; 1 Kings vi. 28).

**Ministering Angels.**—מלאכי שרת = (V)MLAKI (H)ShRTh = Ministering Angels, Servant Angels (Gen. xlviii. 16; Dan. x. 18; Dan. viii. 16; Ps. civ. 4).

**and with these three He founded His dwelling.**

This can be understood in several ways :

(a) (1) The Throne of Glory ;
    (2) Seraphim, Ophanim, and the Holy Animals ;
    (8) the Ministering Angels ;
and with these three He founded His dwelling.

(b) (1) The Throne of Glory ;
    (2) Seraphim ;
    (8) Ophanim, or Holy Animals, to Ministering Angels ;
and with these three He founded His dwelling.

(c) The Throne of Glory.
    (1) Seraphim ;
    (2) Ophanim ; and
    (8) the Holy Animals ; to Ministering Angels ;
and with these three He founded His dwelling.

(d) The Throne of Glory.
   (1) Seraphim ;
   (2) Ophanim, or the Holy Animals ; and
   (3) Ministering Angels ;
and with these three He founded His dwelling.
(e) The Throne of Glory.
   (1) Seraphim ;
   (2) Ophanim ;
   (3) the Holy Animals, or Ministering Angels ;
and with these three He founded His dwelling.

Of these different explanations (a) is the most probable.
The Throne of Glory corresponds to A, the equilibrating power ;
Seraphim, Ophanim, and the Holy Animals correspond to the
three-pointed and fiery Sh ; the Ministering Angels, to the
watery M.

I. 13. **His great name,** Tetragrammaton, the Lord.
(Notes I. 1.)

### TABLE VI.—TETRAGRAMMATON

| Magic. | Equilibrating power. | — *Passive.* | + *Active.* | Result. |
|---|---|---|---|---|
| **IHVH** | I<br>Coition. | H<br>Sight. | V<br>Hearing. | H<br>(Sight.) |
| **R**<br>**A—O**<br>**T**<br>*Passive.* | Love.<br>Wands.<br>(Clubs.)<br>Knight. | Empress.<br>Cups.<br>(Hearts.)<br>Queen. | Emperor.<br>Swords.<br>(Spades.)<br>King. | (Child.)<br>Pantacles.<br>(Diamonds.)<br>Page. |
| △+<br>*Active.* | A<br>Air. | M<br>Water. | Sh<br>Fire. | Mf<br>Earth. |
| Result. | Sylph. | Undine. | Salamander. | Gnome. |

**six ends,** (the Hexagram = MGNf DVD = Shield of David),
the poles of the three dimensions.

**Height, Depth, East, West, North, and South.**    See Notes I. 5.

**upwards.**—מעלה = MOLH =up, upwards.

**stretched backwards,** turned round.

**right.**—ימין = IMINf.

**left.**—שמאל = ShMAL.

This is the only verse in " Sepher Yetzirah " where South precedes North in enumeration of the cardinal points. The content of this verse shows clearly that the words South and North have been exchanged, an error which arose probably with some mediæval transcriber, but is corrected in the present translation. After the Creator had sealed the East He turned round in order to seal the West. In this position North is on His right and South on His left.

The distribution of the different Trigrams in the several texts is as follows :—

| | Text A. | Text B. | Text C. | Text D. | Cimara. | True distribution. |
|---|---|---|---|---|---|---|
| Height . | IHV | IHV | HIV | IHV | IHV | IHV |
| Depth . | IVH | HIV | IVH | IVH | HVI | IVH |
| East . . | HIV | VIH | VIH | HVI | VIH | HIV |
| West . . | HVI | VHI | VHI | HIV | HIV | HVI |
| North . | VHI | HVI | HVI | VIH | VIH | VIH |
| South . | VIH | IVH | IVH | VIH | IVH | VHI |

FIG. 2.

The name of the Lord, IHV, corresponds to Height (" dwelling in the Height," " S. Y.," I. 1). The inf. mood of the verb " to be," היו = HIV, corresponds to East. Future, "shall be," ויה = VIH, corresponds to North. The imperative mood " be," הוי = HVI, answers to West and signifies sorcery. Four Trigrams are found in the 20th line of the Great " Kabalistic Symbol." See also Fig. 2.

I. 14. The first four Sephiroth constitute two groups of transcendental elements : Spirit, Air ; Water, Fire. The last six Sephiroth constitute three groups: the three dimensions of space.

## CHAPTER II

This chapter embodies the secret of the " Great Kabalistic Symbol."

**II. 1. The Twenty-two basal letters** are 22 creating factors or forces. These forces cannot be apprehended by the human Mind unless they are symbolised. In Kabalism their symbols are the 22 Hebrew letters. (Notes I. 2.)

**Three mothers.** See Notes III.

**sibilant,** whistling.

**II. 2. He designed, formed, purified, and weighed them.** This signifies the beauty and harmony of the creation.

**purify.**—צרף = TzRPf =to melt (Bible), to purify (Bible), to unite (Talmud).

**exchange.**—ימר = IMR. (MIMRA =word. VAVMR =: he speaketh.)

**He exchanged them, each one with all.** The combination of symbols or letters. Words. Language.

**II. 3.** The letters are classified according to their sounds : guttural, palatal, lingual, dental, and labial sounds. (Late origin.)

**II. 4, 5. ring,** wheel, circle.

**gate** has the same numerical value as " path " (" S. Y.," I. 1).

**all language.**

**combination of letters.**—ShMf =group of letters, name. *Previous translators, thinking that the Hebrew expression ShMf refers to the holy name of the Lord, inserted the letters of Tetragrammaton amongst the 231 gates and thus constructed the most impossible tables. The expression in question (ShMf) refers to the Wheel with 231 Gates " the Great Kabalistic Symbol."*

## THE GREAT KABALISTIC SYMBOL

### The 231 Gates

Eighteen hundred years ago, when Rabbi Akiba ben Joseph reduced into writing the secret tradition of the Jews in the "Book of Formation," he hesitated to unveil the greatest secret of the Kabala, the Arcanum of the Great Symbol, which had been handed down to him from his forefathers. For this reason he embodied it in a riddle (" S. Y.," II. 4 and 5), which many ancient and modern philosophers have tried in vain to solve. Of all the different tabulations, claiming to be the Great Arcanum of the Kabala, that we have examined, none is correct. The token of the original table ONG and NGO was not to be found in any of them. We have succeeded in solving this riddle. The true Kabalistic Symbol, the Great Master-Key to the theoretical and practical Kabala will be found facing p. 96 of the present translation.

The symbol consists of 21 lines (IHV = 21). Each line contains 22 letters which, by means of 11 circles, are divided in 11 two-letter-words (HV = 11. See Table VI.). The first circle is the perfect circle, because it contains all the letters of the alphabet. The letter A, the equilibrating power, is here combined with all the rest of the letters. For this reason the first circle may be put in rotation while the outer part of the symbol remains fixed. The 10 outer circles do not contain the equilibrating power, and are therefore dependent on the first circle and its movements. The first five of the ten outer circles are more powerful than the last five, because they show 21 (IHV = 21) different forces (letters) against 15 (IH = 15) different forces of the last five circles. Moreover, the letter that starts each circle corresponds in the first six circles of the Symbol to the respective number of the circle. This is not the case with the last five circles (Ch, T, K, M, O).

According to the symbolism of the Kabala we should expect to find the greatest secrets where the most powerful letters are combined. The most powerful letters of the alphabet are the three mothers, A M Sh. The mothers are combined in three places : AM in the 12th line, ASh in the 20th line, and ShM in the 5th line.

AM. In the 12th line we read NGO (plague). If we take the table as a symbol of the Universe, NGO is the idea of suffering. If we take the table as a symbol of Man, NGO is the suffering of Man. How can this suffering be overcome ? Make the apprehensible reflections of the 10 Sephiroth as if your own property. Let the Ego move ten steps forward. Turn the first circle (the innermost circle of the Symbol) ten steps forward and read in the 12th line O(G)N(B)G(A) ; ONG (good, pleasure). This is the token or the key of the Great Symbol and is given in Chapter II. verse 4.

ASh. In the 20th line we read IHV, HIV, and VIH, the Trigrams of the positive trigon of the Hexagram (Fig. 2). VHI, the last seal, is also found equilibrating the first seal IHV.

ShM. In the 5th line we read ShM (combination of letters). This word was used by Rabbi Akiba to signify the Great Master-Key of the Kabala. It has been explained that this word has been misunderstood by students of the Kabala, and owing hereto the riddle has remained unsolved for eighteen centuries.

In the 8rd line, the 4th and 5th circle, we find the name of the Lord, $\pi$ = IH (Notes I. 1), and six circles above this we find conjunctions of equal forces in the 1st, 2nd, 3rd, 4th, 5th, 6th, and 21st lines. These seven conjunctions correspond to the seven double-letters. The seventh (line 21) of these conjunctions corresponds to Th (Saturn); the first (POP) to B (Sun); the second (TzOTz) to G (Moon); the third (QOQ) to D (Mars); the fourth (ROR) to K (Mercurius); the fifth (ShOSh) to P (Jupiter); the sixth (ThOTh) to R (Venus). Compare Table IX.

In the 8th and 9th circles, the 9th to the 19th lines, we find similar conjunctions signifying the 10 Sephiroth.

The Great Symbol of the Kabala embodies the secret of the practical Kabala.

II. 6. **formless.** (Notes I. 11.)

**non-existent.**—אין = AINf = non-existent, the abstract conception of nothingness (Waite); *fine carens* (Rosenroth).

**large columns** (2 Chron. iii. 17), compare the Sephirotic columns or pillars of the Zohar.

**intangible air**, transcendental air. (Notes I. 10.)

**combination of letters.** (Notes II. 5.)

### CHAPTER III

This chapter interprets the three most powerful symbols of the Hebrew alphabet: the three mothers, אמש = A M Sh. The Law of Equilibrium, Table III.

III. 1. This verse contains the fundamental law of the Kabala, the Law of Equilibrium. Sh and M are a pair of scales. In some cases M represents the Good and Sh represents the Evil; in other cases M is the scale of Evil and Sh is the scale of Good. A is always the equilibrating point between the scales. The symbol of this point is the tongue or pointer of the scales. If a finger directs the pointer, the two scales are also directed. If the finger represents the will-power, Good and Evil are directed by the Will. A is a symbol of Man. If he does not use his will-power, the surrounding conditions move him, as the pointer is moved by the weights on the scales; but, if Man uses his will-power, he is able to master the surrounding conditions, as the scales are mastered by the finger which directs the pointer.

III. 2. **six seals.**—(V) מבעות ששׁ = ShSh MBOVTh = six signet-rings, six seals. (Notes I. 13, 14.)

The three mothers are sealed by the Lord (IHV) within the three dimensions of space and thus made apprehensible for the human intellect.

**produced,** born.

**fathers,** patriarchs.

**III. 3. He designed, formed, purified, weighed, and exchanged them.** (Notes II. 2.)

**Universe.**—The world, macrocosm (M).   (ארץ = ARTzf— the Earth.)

**the Year.**—Time (A).

**Man.**—Body, microcosm (Sh).

**male and female** (Gen. i. 27); male (Sh), female (M), love (A).   Table VI.

**III. 5. Air, Water, Fire, and Earth.** (Notes I. 10, 11, 12.)

**heavens.**—שמים = ShMIMf.   (Notes II. 5, ShMf.)

**wind,** atmosphere.

**III. 6. Cold, winter, heat, summer.**

**temperate state.**—רויה = RVIH has a double meaning = temperate state (between heat and cold), moist (between dry and wet) (Ps. xxiii. 5; Ps. lxvi. 12).

**III. 7. chest, body.**

| Man. | | Male. | Female. |
|------|------|-------|---------|
| Head | . . | ShAM | ShMA |
| Chest | . . | AShM | AMSh |
| Belly | . . | MShA | MASh |

Several authors have put forth intentional blinds regarding the three mothers.  אמת = A M Th (Truth) and אמן = A M N (Amen) have been given as mother-letters.  These evasions were prompted probably by the fact that **Sh** relates to Fire, Transmutation, and the Devil.

## CHAPTER IV

In this chapter the holy and the averse heptad are expounded.   Table IV.

**IV. 1. Life.**—חיים = ChIIMf (plur. masc.) =life, support, health.

**Peace.**—שלום = ShLVMf (masc.) =peace, salvation.

**Wisdom.**—חכמה = ChKMH (fem.) =wisdom, learning, art.

**Wealth.**—עשר = OShR (masc.) or OVShR.

**Grace (Beauty).**—חן = ChNf or חין = ChINf (masc.).

**Fruitfulness.**—זרע = ZRO (masc.) =fruitfulness, seed, sperm.

**Dominion.**—וממשלה = VMMShLH (fem.) =dominion, power.

**IV. 3. permutation,** contrast.

**Death.**—מות = MVTh (masc.).

**Misfortune.**—רע = RO (masc.) =misfortune, evil, weakness, illness.

**Folly.**—אולת = AVLTh.

**Poverty.**—עוני = OVNI or עני = ONI (masc.).

**Ugliness.**—כיעור = KIOVR (masc.).

**Devastation.**—שממה = ShMMH (fem.) =devastation, desolation.

**Slavery.**—עבדות = OBDVTh (fem.).

IV. 4. **Height, Depth, East, West, North, and South.** (Notes I. 5; Notes III. 2, six seals).

(the) **Holy Palace.**—היכל הקודש = (V)HIKL HQVDSh. (Jerusalem or Zion, where Man can communicate with God.) It corresponds to the mouth. (According to Zohar it relates to the organ of sexual intercourse.)

IV. 5. **examine and search out by means of them.** This refers to Kabalistic Astrology and its associated arts.

**throne, place.**

IV. 6. **He designed, formed, purified, weighed, and exchanged them.** (Notes II. 2.)

**Universe, the Year, Man.** (Notes III. 3.)

**seven weeks.** Probably the seven weeks between Passover and the Feast of Pentecost.

IV. 7–14. The order of the planets is according to Text A. (See p. 67.) The other texts give: Saturn, Jupiter, Mars, Sun, Venus, Mercurius, Moon; or Saturn, Mars, Mercurius, Sun, Jupiter, Venus, Moon; or Sun, Venus, Mercurius, Moon, Saturn, Jupiter, Mars. The planets are enumerated (verse 7) in an order that corresponds to their velocity. First Saturn, which is the slowest of the seven planets, then Jupiter and Mars. The apparent velocity of the Sun lies between the velocity of Mars and that of Venus. After Venus comes Mercurius, and last, the swiftest of them all, the Moon. Each of these planets has two poles, one negative and one positive; the negative pole corresponds to the evil foundation and the positive to the good foundation. These "twice seven" different powers are directed by the zodiacal signs. In Aries they are directed according to the constant virtues of that sign; and so on through all the 12 signs of the zodiac. Thus we get: $2 \times 7 \times 12 = 168$. 168 different planetary influences in the Universe. Table VII. shows these 168 influences. The planets are inserted in the table according to the order of their velocity, starting at the upper left-hand corner and proceeding downwards. The table consists of

7 columns. The planets of the uppermost row correspond to the days of the week, and the 24 influences of each column correspond to the hours of the day. Thus the Hebrew letters, products in Time—otherwise, in the year—are deducted from their products in the Universe (the planets and the zodiacal signs). It is interesting to note that Saturday precedes Sunday in the enumeration of the days of the week. Compare this with the seven conjunctions of forces in the Great Symbol of the Kabala (see plate facing p. 24). There is a close spiritual relation between the "last" and the "first," in this case between Th (Saturn) and B (Sun). Saturday is the Sabbath of the Jews and Sunday is the Sabbath of the Christians. If we compare the Tarot-correspondences of Th and B, we shall reach the same result. The head of "the hanged man" signifies the Sun; the gallows, in the form of a Hebrew Th, signifies the orbit of Saturn. Compare the 20th Path in "The 32 Paths of Wisdom" (Notes VI. 11).

|  | Text A. | Durville : French edition, 1913. | Bresslau Dictionary. |
|---|---|---|---|
| Saturn . . . | ShBThAI | ShBThI    nr. 1 | |
| Jupiter . . | TzDQ | TzDQ      „   5 | |
| Mars . . . | MADIMf | NVGH      „   2 | MZL. |
| Sun . . . | ChMCh | ChMCh     „   4 | (ShMSh). |
| Venus . . . | NVGH | KVKB      „   6 | KKB NGH. |
| Mercury . . | KVKB | MADIMf    „   8 | KKB. |
| Moon . . . | LBNH | LBGH      „   7 | IRCh. |

**right eye.**—עין ימין = OINf IMINf (fem.).

**left eye.**—עין שמאל = OINf ShMAL (fem.).

**right ear.**—אוזן (אזן) ימין = AVZNf IMINf (AZNf IMINf) (masc.).

**left ear.**—אוזן (אזן) שמאל = AVZNf ShMAL (AZNf ShMAL) (masc.).

**right nostril.**—נחיר ימין = NChIR IMIN (masc.).

**left nostril.**—נחיר שמאל = NChIR ShMAL (masc.).

**mouth.**—פה = PH (common gender).

IV. 15. **Holy Palace.** (Notes IV. 4.)

12 enumerations (corresponding to the 12 simple-letters), 11 heptads and the Holy Palace. 11×7=77; 77+1=78; 78 is the number of cards in the Tarot.

## TABLE VII.—THE CHALDEAN CALENDAR

| Saturday. | Sunday. | Monday. | Tuesday. | Wednesday. | Thursday. | Friday. | Hours. |
|---|---|---|---|---|---|---|---|
| Th H | B V | G Ch | D I | K L | P S | R Tz | 12–1 a.m. |
| P H | R V | Th Ch | B I | G L | D S | Kf Tzf | 1–2 a.m. |
| D H | K V | P Ch | R I | Th N | B S | G Tz | 2–3 a.m. |
| B H | G V | D Ch | K I | Pf Nf | R S | Th Tz | 3–4 a.m. |
| R H | Th Z | B Ch | G I | D N | K S | Pf Tzf | 4–5 a.m. |
| K H | P Z | R Ch | Th I | B N | G S | D Tz | 5–6 a.m. |
| G H | D Z | K Ch | P I | R N | Th O | B Tz | 6–7 a.m. |
| Th H | B Z | G Ch | D I | Kf Nf | P O | R Tz | 7–8 a.m. |
| P H | R Z | Th T | B I | G N | D O | Kf Tzf | 8–9 a.m. |
| D H | K Z | P T | R I | Th N | B O | G Tz | 9–10 a.m. |
| B H | G Z | D T | K I | Pf Nf | R O | Th Q | 10–11 a.m. |
| R H | Th Z | B T | G I | D N | K O | P Q | 11–12 a.m. |
| K H | P Z | R T | Th L | B N | G O | D Q | 12–1 p.m. |
| G H | D Z | K T | P L | R N | Th O | B Q | 1–2 p.m. |
| Th V | B Z | G T | D L | Kf Nf | P O | R Q | 2–3 p.m. |
| P V | R Z | Th T | B L | G N | D O | K Q | 3–4 p.m. |
| D V | K Z | P T | R L | Th S | B O | G Q | 4–5 p.m. |
| B V | G Z | D T | K L | P S | R O | Th Q | 5–6 p.m. |
| R V | Th Ch | B T | G L | D S | K O | P Q | 6–7 p.m. |
| K V | P Ch | R T | Th L | B S | G O | D Q | 7–8 p.m. |
| G V | D Ch | K T | P L | R S | Th Tz | B Q | 8–9 p.m. |
| Th V | B Ch | G T | D L | K S | Pf Tzf | R Q | 9–10 p.m. |
| P V | R Ch | Th I | B L | G S | D Tz | K Q | 10–11 p.m. |
| D V | K Ch | P I | R L | Th S | B Tz | G Q | 11–12 p.m. |

4

IV. 16.

| | | |
|---|---|---|
| 1 stone : | 1 | =1 house. |
| 2 stones : | 1×2 | =2 houses. |
| 3 stones : | 1×2×3 | =6 houses. |
| 4 stones : | 1×2×3×4 | =24 houses. |
| 5 stones : | 1×2×3×4×5 | =120 houses. |
| 6 stones : | 1×2×3×4×5×6 | =720 houses. |
| 7 stones : | 1×2×3×4×5×6×7 | =5040 houses. |
| 8 stones : | 1×2×3×4×5×6×7×8 | =40320 houses. |
| 9 stones : | 1×2×3×4×5×6×7×8×9 | =362880 houses. |
| 10 stones : | 1×2×3×4×5×6×7×8×9×10 | =3628800 houses. |
| 11 stones : | 1×2×3×4×5×6×7×8×9×10×11 | =39916800 houses. |
| 12 stones : | 1×2×3×4×5×6×7×8×9×10×11×12 | =479001600 houses. |

**stones** (letters).
**houses** (words).

## CHAPTER V

This chapter elucidates the secrets of the constant dodecad. Table V.

**V. 1. Sight.**—ראיה = RAIH (fem.).

**Hearing.**—שמעה = ShMOH (ShMO) (verb) =hear.

**Smell.**—ריח = (RICh) RIChH (RIChA) (masc.).

**Speech.**—שיחה = ShIChH (ShChH) (ShVChH) (fem.) =speech, low speech.

**Taste.**—(לעט) לעיטה = LOITH (LOT) (fem.) =eating, digestion, eating and drinking, savour.

**Coition.**—תשמיש = ThShMISh (masc.).

**Work.**—(עשה) מעשה = MOShH (OShH) (masc.) = work, action, employment.

**Movement.**—(הילוך) הלוך = HLVKf (HILVKf) (masc. = movement, walking, motion.

**Wrath.**—רוגז = RVGZ (masc.) = wrath, anger, excitement.

**Mirth.**—(שחק) שחוק = ShChVQ (masc.) = mirth, laughter, idolatry, sin.

**Meditation.**—הרהור = HRHVR (HRHR) (HIRHVR) (masc.) = meditation, thought, mind (Pistorius); suspicion (Postellus); imagination (Westcott).

**Sleep.**—(שינא) (שכה) שינה = ShINH (ShNH) (ShINA) (fem.) = sleep; (ShINA or ShIN (masc.) =urine.). Compare Table I.

These 12 words stand, according to several old Kabalists, in a certain relation to PShVTVTh.

**V. 2. oblique.**—אלכסון=ALKSVNf.

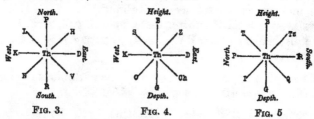

FIG. 3.            FIG. 4.            FIG. 5

**stretch out,** stretch themselves out.

**V. 3. He designed, formed, purified, exchanged, and weighed them.** See Notes II. 2.

**zodiacal sign.**—MZL =place of ascending, shelter, fortune, fate, zodiacal sign.

**V. 4. Aries.**—טלה = TLH =ram.
**Taurus.**—שור = ShVR =bull.
**Gemini.**—תאומים = ThAVMIMf =twins.
**Cancer.**—סרטן = SRTNf =crab.
**Leo.**—אריה = ARIH =lion.
**Virgo.**—בתולה = BThVLH =virgin.
**Libra.**—מאזנים = MAZNIMf =scales.
**Scorpio.**—עקרב = OQRB =scorpion.
**Sagittarius.**—קשת = QShTh =arch.
**Capricornus.**—גדי = GDI =goat.
**Aquarius.**—דלי = DLI =pail.
**Pisces.**—דגים = DGIMf =fishes.

**V. 5. Twelve months in the Year:** ניסן = NISNf, אייר = AIIR, סיון = SIVNf, תמוז = ThMVZ, אב = AB, אלול = ALVL, תשרי = ThShRI, מרחשון = MRChShVNf (Cimara gives חשון = ChShVNf), כסלו = KSLV (Cimara gives כסליו = KSLIV), טבת = TBTh, שבט = ShBT, אדר = ADR.

**V. 6. right hand.**—יד ימין = ID IMINf.
**left hand.**—יד שמאל = ID ShMAL. (ID, masc. *or* fem.)
**right foot.**—רגל ימין=RGL IMINf.
**left foot.**—רגל שמאל = RGL ShMAL. (RGL, fem.)
**right kidney.**—כוליא ימין = KVLIA IMINf (KVLIIA IMINf) = right kidney, right testicle.
**left kidney.** — כוליא שמאל = KVLIA ShMAL (KVLIIA ShMAL) =left kidney, left testicle. (KVLIA, fem.)
**liver.**—כבד = KBD = weight, pressure (masc.); heaviness, seat of melancholy, liver (masc. *or* fem.).

**spleen.**—טחל‎ = TChL (TChVL) (masc.). ("Having had their milt cut as fast runners." Talmud.)

**gall.**—מרה‎ = MRH =bitter taste, poison, gall, pick, to be fat, to be disobedient (רוש‎ = RVSh, gall) (מרהביא‎ = MRHBIA, pride, haughtiness).

The following three words are very dubious: והמסס‎ = VHMSS, וקיבה‎ = VQIBH, וקורקבן‎ = VQVRQBNf.

**stomach.**—HMSS (MSS) =intestine, gut, bowel; private, secret, hidden; liquid (masc.); to melt, to dissolve; stomach (masc.); the first stomach of ruminants.

**colon.**—QIBH (QBH) =stomach (fem.); craw of birds; the fourth stomach of ruminants, the idea includes also the fat in or about this stomach; (HQBH) rennet, used to curdle milk.

**bowel.**—QVRQBNf =stomach in Man; craw of birds; rectum in Man (masc.).

*The translation of these dubious words according to :*

| | | |
|---|---|---|
| Pistorius | . . | colon, coagulum, et ventriculus. |
| | | (*large intestine, spleen, and stomach.*) |
| Postellus | . . | colon, coagulum, et ventriculus. |
| Rittangelius | . . | intestina, sesica, et arteriæ. |
| | | (*intestines, bladder, and arteries.*) |
| Cimara | . . | les intestins, le colon, l'estomac. |
| Goldschmidt | . . | Darm, Magen, Mastdarm. |
| Westcott | . . | private parts, stomach, intestines. |

In an old commentary we read : " *Two discontented or insulting: the liver, the gall. Two jolly or laughing : the colon, the spleen. Two advising : the kidneys. Two taking advice : the stomach, the bowels (rectum). Two robbing : the hands. Two hunting : the feet.*"

*Note.*—" *colon,*" " *stomach,*" *and* " *bowels.*"

**God.**—אלהים‎ = ALHIMf. (Notes I. 1.)

V. 7–18. See Notes V. 1–6.

V. 19. **as a wall.**—(a circle) like a city wall, the zodiacal circle.

There is a constant strife amongst the 12 simple-letters (the zodiacal signs). They are all of the same strength and arranged round a circle. The directions and manifestations of these forces cannot be influenced or changed in any way, but they themselves influence other forces, *i.e.,* the 7 double-letters corresponding to the planets.

## CHAPTER VI

This chapter explains the relation in which the triad, the heptad, and the dodecad stand to each other.

VI. 1. **that are three fathers**—means that copulation of different sex qualities was not used by the Creator when the essences of Fire, Air, and Water were created.

VI. 2. **the Holy.**—וְהַקְדוֹשׁ = VHQDVSh. About the names of the Lord, see Notes I. 1.

*The first two verses of this chapter constitute in the texts the end of Chapter V. We have ventured to transfer them to this chapter on account of their contents.*

VI. 3. **From the three He founded His dwelling** (Notes I. 12).

VI. 5. **twelve oblique angles.**—This expression is misplaced. " Twelve zodiacal signs " would be more reasonable.

VI. 6. **the dodecad.**
HVZChTILNSOTzQ.

12 forces arranged in a circle make one unity. This unity plus the 12 individual forces make 13.

The finals of the heptad, KfPf $=500+800+1300$ ; 13.
אֶחָד $=$ AChD (Deut. vi. 4, One, Unity) $=13$.
בְּרֵאשִׁית $=$ BRAShITh (the first word in the Hebrew Bible, meaning " In the beginning ") $=913$ ; $9+1+3=13$.
אַהֲבָה $=$ AHBH (Love) $=13$.

**the heptad.**
BGDKPRTh $=2+3+4+20+80+200+400=709$ ;
$$7+0+9=16 ; \quad 1+6=7.$$
The finals of the dodecad, NfTzf $=700+900=1600$ ; $1+6=7$.
The sum of the squares on the 10 Sephiroth is equal to 385 :
$$1+2^2+3^2+4^2+5^2+6^2+7^2+8^2+9^2+10^2=1+4+9+16$$
$$+25+36+49+64+81+100=385; \quad 3+8+5=16; \quad 1+6=7.$$
שְׁכִינָה $=$ ShKINH (The Divine Majesty) $=300+20+10+50$
$$+5=385; \quad 3+8+5=16; \quad 1+6=7.$$
יָבֹא שִׁילֹה $=$ IBA ShILH (Gen. xlix. 10, " Shiloh shall come ")
$$=358; \quad 3+5+8=16; \quad 1+6=7.$$
מָשִׁיחַ $=$ MShICh (Messiah) $=358$ ; $3+5+8=16$ ; $1+6=7$.
עֵץ $=$ OTz (Gen. ii. 9, " The Tree of good and evil ")
$$=70+90=160; \quad 1+6=7.$$

**the triad.**

אמש = AMSh =341 ; 3+4+1 =8.

שדי = ShDI (" Almighty," name of God)=314 ; 3+1+4 =8.

מטטרון = MTTRVN ("Angel of the Presence," "World Prince " ; Zohar)=814 ; 3+1+4 =8.

והנה שלשה = VHNH ShLShH (Gen. xviii. 2, " And lo, three men ") =701 ; 7+1=8.

אלו מיכאל גבריאל ורפאל = ALV MIKAL GBRIAL VRPAL (" These are Michael, Gabriel, and Raphael ") =701 ; 7+1=8.

**the dragon.**—תלי = ThLI =the dragon (which encircles the Universe) (12 simple-letters).

**sphere.**—גלגל = GLGL =(celestial) sphere (7 double-letters).

*The sphere precedes the dragon in the text, but as the dragon corresponds to the Universe we have changed the order.*

**VI. 7. Notes III. 5.**

**VI. 8.**      TABLE VIII.—TO BE

| The King. | Dragon (H). | Sphere (I). | Heart (V). |
|---|---|---|---|
| Universe (M): | 12 zodiacal signs. | 7 planets. | Earth. |
| The Year. (A): | 12 months. | 7 days. | Temperate state. |
| Man. (Sh): | 12 leading members. | 7 gateways. | Head. (Reason.) |

" **The dragon** " in the Universe is like a king on his throne, because everything which is encircled by the Odic dragon (the zodiac) is ruled by the signs of the zodiac, as a country is ruled by its king.

" **the sphere** " in the Year is like a king in a province.—The kingdom of "the Year " has 52 provinces, the 52 weeks. The present week is like a king in his province.

" **the heart** " (in Man) is like a king in warfare.—The human intelligence is always in warfare against ignorance and superstition.

**VI. 9. God.**—האלהים = HALHIMf. (Notes I. 1.)

**the good marks out the evil, and the evil marks out the good,** the evil is distinguished by means of the good, and the good is distinguished by means of the evil.

" good " is reserved for the good ones, and " evil " is reserved for the evil ones.

**" good."**—טוב = TVB, טובה =TVBH =good (end).

**" evil."**—רע =RO, רעה = ROH =evil (end).

**VI. 10. himself,** *or* herself.

**merited,** sanctified, made happy, exonerated.

**loaded with guilt,** excommunicated, made unhappy, accused. (Notes III. 1.)

**VI. 11. between the two groups,** *or* amongst them.

Amongst the seven doubles, either B or Th is the equilibrating power (see the 20th path of " The 82 Paths of Wisdom "). If B (Sun) equilibrates : Th (Saturn), P (Jupiter), and D (Mars) constitute one group ; R (Venus), K (Mercurius), and G (Moon) are the other group, or—G D K one group, and P R Th the other. If Th (Saturn) equilibrates : D, P, and B constitute one group, R, K, and G the other group, or—B R P one group, and G D K the other. (Notes IV. 7–14.)

In the first line of Table IX. we find the doubles in an order that corresponds to their velocity in the Universe. In the second line we find them in an order that corresponds to their enumeration in the Year (the days of the week). If Th (Saturn) is equilibrating, the spiritual focus A (*see our notes to the 20th path of " The 32 Paths of Wisdom "*) predominates; the material focus B (Sun) is then of lesser importance. This is symbolised in the third and fourth line of our table. The third line is deducted from the first line in the following manner : Let B and Th in the first line exchange their positions. Th is now the equilibrating power and the polarity of the line is changed —it is written in the opposite direction. The fourth line stands in the same relation to the third as the second to the first. About the finals, see Table X.

**VI. 13.** This is the most clumsy of all the spurious passages in " Sepher Yetzirah."

**VI. 15.** אהיה = **AHIH**=I am (Exod. iii. 14). 1+5+10+5 =21. (Notes II. 4, 5.)

TABLE IX.—THE EQUILIBRIUM OF THE 7 DOUBLES

| | M. | A. | Sh. |
|---|---|---|---|
| **H** | ♄ Th　♃ P　♂ D<br>Pf<br>Ψ | ☉ B | ♀ R　☿ K　☽ G<br>Kf<br>♅ |
| **I** | ♃ P　♀ R　♄ Th<br>Pf<br>Ψ | ☉ B | ☽ G　♂ D　☿ K<br>Kf<br>♅ |
| **H** | G ☽　K ☿　R ♀<br>Kf<br>♅ | Th ♄ | D ♂　P ♃　B ☉<br>Pf<br>Ψ |
| **I** | K ☿　D ♂　G ☽<br>Kf<br>♅ | Th ♄ | B ☉　R ♀　P ♃<br>Pf<br>Ψ |

שדי = **ShDI** = Almighty (Gen. xvii. 1 ; Ezek. i. 24).

אדני = **ADNI** = God. (The name of the Lord that may be pronounced.) (Jud. i. 5.)

About the other names of God, see Notes I. 1.

**designed**, written.

**He made three numbers of them.** See the dodecad, the heptad, and the triad (Notes VI. 6).

VI. 16.—**the Lord of the Universe.**—אדון עלים = OLIMf ADVNf.

**bosom**, lap.

**the Lord.**—IHVH. (Notes I. 1.)

**between his hands.** A word-for-word translation would be : " between the ten fingers of his (two) hands."

**between his feet.** A word-for-word translation would be : " between the ten toes of his (two) feet." (Notes I. 3.)

**(the) Thora.**—תורה = (H)ThVRH = Pentateuch.

**the Holy.**—והקדש = VHQDVSh.

## TABLE X.—THE 5 FINALS

| ⛤ | Mother. | Doubles. | | Simples. | |
|---|---|---|---|---|---|
| | Mf. *The essence of Earth.* | Kf. | Pf. | Nf. | Tzf. |
| Their Foundation: | Result. | *Mystical Life and mystical Death.* | Dominion over and Slavery under unknown forces. | Movement in unknown dimensions. | Meditation (*the body paralysed*). |
| Universe (M): | ▽ Earth. | ♅ (Uranus). | ♆ (Neptune). | ♏ (Scorpio). | ♒ (Aquarius). |
| The Year (A): | Cold. | Wednesdays *when ☉ in ♏ or ☉ in ♒* | Thursdays *when ☉ in ♒ or ☉ in ♏* | (*Oct. 23–Nov. 22*) *when ♅ in ♏ or ♆ in ♏* Marḥešvan. | (*Jan. 20–Feb. 19*) *when ♆ in ♒ or ♅ in ♒* Šebath. |
| Man (Sh): | (Child.) | 8th gateway. | 9th gateway. | Milt. | Poisonous fluids. |

# THE 32 PATHS OF WISDOM

*THE author of this tract is unknown. Judging from the style of the treatise it is of considerably later date than " Sepher Yetzirah." As there are several extant versions which differ in various points, the tabulation of Paths and their titles will be given according to Comtesse Calomira de Cimara, and the translation of the tract according to Waite and Westcott. The correspondences with Hebrew letters and the Tarot symbols have been established on our own part.*

(THE TRANSCENDENTAL DECAD)

The **first path** is called the **Mystical Intelligence.**

הנתיב ה א נקרא שכל מופלא.¹

HNThIB H " A " NQRA ShKL MVPLA.

(Sephira 1. In Tarot, the four **Aces.**)

" The first path is called the Admirable Intelligence, the Supreme Crown. It is the light which imparts understanding of the beginning which is without beginning, and this also is the First Splendour. No created being can attain to its essence." (Waite.)

The **second path** is called the **Illuminating Intelligence.**

HNThIB H " B " NQRA ShKL מזהיר = MZHIR.

(Sephira 2. In Tarot, the four **Twos.**)

" The second path is called the Illuminating Intelligence. It is the Crown of Creation and the splendour of the Supreme Unity, to which it is most near in proximity. It is exalted above every head, and is distinguished by Kabalists as the Second Splendour." (Waite.)

The **third path** is called the **Sanctifying Intelligence.**

HNThIB H " G " NQRA ShKL מקורש = MQVDSh.

(Sephira 3. In Tarot, the four **Threes.**)

" The third path is called the Sanctifying Intelligence, and it is the foundation of Primordial Wisdom, termed the Creation of Faith. Its roots are AMKf. It is the mother of Faith, which indeed emanates therefrom." (Waite.)

¹ In the subsequent enumeration of Paths only the variant qualifications of Intelligence are given in Hebrew lettering.

The **fourth path** is called the **Receptacular Intelligence.**
HNThIB H " D " NQRA ShKL קבוע = QBVO.
(Sephira **4.** In Tarot, the four **Fours.**)

" The fourth path is called the Arresting or Receiving Intelligence, because it arises like a boundary to receive the emanations of the higher intelligences which are sent down to it. Herefrom all spiritual virtues emanate by the way of subtlety, which itself emanates from the Supreme Crown." (Waite.)

" The fourth path is named Measuring, Cohesive, or Receptacular ; and is so called because it contains all the holy powers, and from it emanate all spiritual virtues with the most exalted essences ; they emanate one from the other by the power of the primordial emanation." (Westcott.)

(" *The Supreme Crown* " *and* " *the primordial emanation* " *signify Sephira 1.*)

The **fifth path** is called the **Radical or Rooted Intelligence.**
HNThIB H " H " NQRA ShKL נשרש = NShRSh.
(Sephira **5.** In Tarot, the four **Fives.**)

" The fifth path is called the Radical Intelligence, because it is more akin than any other to the Supreme Unity and emanates from the depths of the Primordial Wisdom." (Waite.)

" . . . from the primordial depths of Chokmah." (Westcott.)

(" *The Primordial Wisdom* " *and* " *Chokmah* " *signify Sephiroth 2.*)

The **sixth path** is called the **Intelligence of Separated Emanation.**
HNThIB H " V " NQRA ShKL שפע נבדל = ShPO NBDL.
(Sephira **6.** In Tarot, the four **Sixes.**)

" The sixth path is called the Intelligence of Mediating Influence, because the flux of the emanations is multiplied therein. It communicates this affluence to those blessed men who are united with it." (Waite.)

" . . . It causes that influence to flow into all the reservoirs of the Blessings with which these themselves are united." (Westcott.)

The **seventh path** is called the **Hidden Intelligence.**
HNThIB H " Z " NQRA ShKL נסתר = NSThR.
(Sephira **7.** In Tarot, the four **Sevens.**)

" The seventh path is called the Hidden Intelligence, because it pours out a brilliant splendour on all intellectual virtues which are beheld with the eyes of the spirit and by the ecstasy of faith." (Waite.)

The **eighth path** is called the **Perfect Intelligence.**
HNThIB H " Ch " NQRA ShKL שלם = ShLMf.
(Sephira **8.** In Tarot, the four **Eights.**)
" The eighth path is called the Perfect and Absolute Intelligence. The preparation of principles emanates therefrom.[1] The roots to which it adheres are in the depths of the Sphere Magnificence, from the very substance of which it emanates." (Waite.)

The **ninth path** is called the **Purified Intelligence.**
HNThIB H " T " NQRA ShKL שהור = THVR.
(Sephira **9.** In Tarot, the four **Nines.**)
" The ninth path is called the Purified Intelligence. It purifies the numerations, prevents and stays the fracture of their images, for it establishes their unity to preserve them from destruction and division by their union with itself." (Waite.)
" The ninth path is named the Purified Intelligence. It purifies the numerations, proves and corrects the designing of their representations, it disposes their unity with which they are combined without diminution or division." (Westcott.)

The **tenth path** is called the **Resplendent Intelligence.**
HNThIB H " I " NQRA ShKL מתנוצע = MThNVTzO.
(Sephira **10.** In Tarot, the four **Tens.**)
" The tenth path is called Resplendent Intelligence, because it is exalted above every head and has its seat in Binah;[2] it enlightens the fire of all lights and emanates the power of the principle of forms." (Waite.)
" . . . causes a supply of influence to emanate from the Prince of Countenances." (Westcott.)

(THE PERFECT TRIAD)

The **eleventh path** is called the **Fiery Intelligence.**
HNThIB I " A " NQRA ShKL מצודצה = MTzVChTzCh.
(The mother-letter **Sh.** Fire △. In Tarot, the **Devil.**)
" The eleventh path is called the Fiery Intelligence. It is the veil placed before the dispositions and order of the superior and inferior causes. Whosoever possesses this path is in the

---

[1] " . . . It is the means of the primordial. . . . " (Westcott.)
[2] Binah=Understanding=Sephira 3.

enjoyment of great dignity; to possess it is to be face to face with the Cause of Causes." (Waite.)

"The eleventh path is named the Fiery Intelligence. It is the essence of that curtain which is placed close to the order of disposition, and this is a special dignity given to it that it may be able to stand before the face of the Cause of Causes." (Westcott.)

(The secret of Transmutation is communicated from this path (Sh). *According to Éliphas Lévi ("La Clef des Grand Mystères," p. 284), this secret belongs to the 31st path. He applied the Hebrew letters in their "alphabetical order" to the 22 last paths. This manner of application is, however, entirely wrong.*)

The **twelfth path** is called the **Intelligence of Transparency.**
HNThIB I " B " NQRA ShKL בדהיר = BHIR.
(The mother-letter **M.** Water ▽. In Tarot, the **World.**)
"The twelfth path is called the Intelligence of the Light,[1] because it is the image of magnificence. It is said to be the source of vision in those who behold apparitions." (Waite.)

The **thirteenth path** is called the **Conductive Intelligence of Unity.**
HNThIB I " G " NQRA ShKL מנהיג = MNHIG (or האחדות = HAChDVTh).
(The mother-letter **A.** Air △. In Tarot, the **Magician.**)
"The thirteenth path is called the Inductive Intelligence of Unity. It is the substance of glory, and it manifests truth to every spirit." (Waite.)
". . . It is the consummation of the truth of individual spiritual things." (Westcott.)

(No magical work can be accomplished without communication with this path. It is the equilibrating power and the source of volition. It is the spiritual focus of gravitation and the directing force. The Conductive Intelligence is always accompanied by Responsibility. These two ideas stand in direct proportion to each other.)

(THE HOLY AND THE AVERSE HEPTAD)

The **fourteenth path** is called the **Luminous Intelligence.**
HNThIB I " D " NQRA ShKL מאיר = MAIR.
(The double-letter **B.** Sun ⊙. In Tarot, the **Sun.**)
"The fourteenth path is called the Illuminating Intelligence.

---

[1] ". . . The Intelligence of Transparency. . . ." (Westcott.)

It is the institutor of arcana, the foundation of holiness."
(Waite.)
(The path of Wisdom and Folly.)

The **fifteenth path** is called the **Constituting Intelligence.**
HNThIB T " V " NQRA ShKL מעמיד = MOMID.
(The double-letter **G.** Moon ☽. In Tarot, the **Moon.**)
" The fifteenth path is called the Constituting Intelligence,
because it constitutes creation in the darkness of the world.[1]
According to the philosophers, it is itself that darkness men-
tioned by Scripture (Job xxxviii. 9), cloud and the envelope
thereof." (Waite.)
(The path of Wealth and Poverty.)

The **sixteenth path** is called the **Eternal Intelligence.**
HNThIB I " V " NQRA ShKL נצחי = NTzChI.
(The double-letter **D.** Mars ♂. In Tarot, the **Chariot.**)
" The sixteenth path is called the Triumphant and Eternal
Intelligence, the delight of glory, the paradise of pleasure pre-
pared for the just." (Waite.)
(The path of Fruitfulness and Devastation.)

The **seventeenth path** is called the **Sensible and Disposing
Intelligence.**
HNThIB I " Z " NQRA ShKL ההרגש = HHRGSh.
(The double-letter **K.** Mercurius ☿. In Tarot, **Death.**)
" The seventeenth path is called the Disposing Intelligence.
It disposes the devout to perseverance, and thus prepares them
to receive the Holy Spirit." [2] (Waite.)
(The path of Life and Death.)

The **eighteenth path** is called the **Emanative Intelligence or
House of Influence.**
HNThIB I " Ch " NQRA ShKL בית השפע = BITh HShPO.
(The double-letter **P.** Jupiter ♃. In Tarot, the **Hierophant.**)
" The eighteenth path is called the Intelligence or House
of Influence,[3] and thence are drawn the arcana and the concealed
meanings which repose in the shadow thereof." (Waite.)
(The path of Dominion and Slavery.)

[1] " . . . It constitutes the substance of creations in pure darkness. . . ."
(Westcott.)
[2] " . . . It is called the foundation of excellence in the state of higher
things." (*Added by* Westcott.)
[3] " . . . By the greatness of whose abundance the influx of good things
upon created beings is increased. . . ." (*Added by* Westcott.)

The **nineteenth path** is called the **Intelligence of the Secret of Spiritual Activities.**

HNThIB I " T " NQRA ShKL המפעולט סרד = SVD HPOVLVT.

(The double-letter **R.** Venus ♀. In Tarot, the **Star.**)

" The nineteenth path is called the Intelligence of the Secret (or) of (all) spiritual activities. The fullness which it receives derives from the highest benediction and the supreme glory." (Waite.)

(The path of Peace and Misfortune.)

The **twentieth path** is called the **Intelligence of Will.**

HNThIB " K " NQRA ShKL חרצון = HRTzVNf.

(The double-letter **Th.** Saturn ♄. In Tarot, the **Hanged Man.**)

" The twentieth path is called the Intelligence of Will. It prepares all created beings, each individually, for the demonstration of the existence of the primordial glory." (Waite.)

(The path of Grace and Ugliness.)

(Th (Saturn), the seventh and last of the heptad, is like an ellipse having one of its foci in A (the equilibrating power, the Spiritual Sun) and the other in B (the Sun). The double-letters G (Moon), D (Mars), K (Mercurius), P (Jupiter), and R (Venus) are always within the limits of this ellipse. Th and B (the first of the heptad) stand in a very close spiritual relation to each other.) (Notes IV. 7–14; VI. 11.)

(THE CONSTANT DODECAD)

The **twenty-first path** is called the **Intelligence of Desire.**

HNThIB K " A " NQRA ShKL המבוקש חחפץ = HChPTzf HMBVQSh.

(The simple-letter **H.** Aries ♈. In Tarot, the **Empress.**)

" The twenty-first path is called the Rewarding Intelligence of those who seek.[1] It receives the divine influence, and it influences by its benediction all existing things." (Waite.)

(The path of Sight.)

The **twenty-second path** is called the **Faithful Intelligence.**

HNThIB K " B " NQRA ShKL נאמן = NAMNf.

(The simple-letter **V.** Taurus ♉. In Tarot, the **Emperor.**)

" The twenty-second path is called the Faithful Intelligence, because spiritual virtues are deposited and augment therein,

[1] " The twenty-first path is named the Conciliating Intelligence. . . ." (Westcott.)

until they pass to those who dwell under the shadow thereof."
(Waite.)

" The twenty-second path is named the Faithful Intelligence,
by it spiritual virtues are increased, and all dwellers on earth
are merely under its shadow." (Westcott.)

(The path of Hearing.)

The **twenty-third path** is called the **Stable Intelligence.**
HNThIB K " G " NQRA ShKL קיים = QIIMf.
(The simple-letter **Z.** Gemini Ⅱ. In Tarot, the **High
Priestess.**)

" The twenty-third path is called the Stable Intelligence.
It is the source of consistency in all the numerations." (Waite.)
(The path of Smell.)

The **twenty-fourth path** is called the **Imaginative Intelligence.**
HNThIB K " D " NQRA ShKL דמיוני = DMIVNI.
(The simple-letter **Ch.** Cancer ♋. In Tarot, **Strength.**)

" The twenty-fourth path is called the Imaginative Intelligence. It is the ground of similarity in the likeness of beings
who are created to its agreement after its aspects." (Waite.)
(The path of Speech.)

The **twenty-fifth path** is called the **Intelligence of Temptation
or Trial.**
HNThIB K " H " NQRA ShKL נסיוני = NSIVNI.
(The simple-letter **T.** Leo ♌. In Tarot, **Temperance.**)

" The twenty-fifth path is called the Intelligence of Temptation or Trial, because it is the first temptation by which God
tests the devout." (Waite.)
(The path of Eating *and Drinking*.)

The **twenty-sixth path** is called the **Renewing Intelligence.**
HNThIB K " V " NQRA ShKL מחדש = MChDSh (*or*
מחודש = MChVDSh).
(The simple-letter **I.** Virgo ♍. In Tarot, the **Lovers.**)

" The twenty-sixth path is called the Renewing Intelligence,
for thereby God—blessed be He !—reneweth all which is capable
of renovation in the creation of the world." [1] (Waite.)
(The path of Coition.)

The **(twenty-seventh) path** is called the **Natural Intelligence.**

[1] " . . . reneweth all the changing things which are renewed by the
creation of the world." (Westcott.)

HNThIB (K " Z ") NQRA ShKL מוטבע = MVTBO.
(The simple-letter L. Libra ♎. In Tarot, **Justice.**)
" The (twenty-seventh) path is called the Natural Intelligence, whereby the nature of everything found in the orb of the sun is completed and perfected." (Waite.)
" The twenty-seventh path is the Exciting Intelligence, and it is so called because through it is consummated and perfected the nature of every existent being under the orb of the sun, in perfection." (Westcott.)
(The path of Work.)
(*Comtesse Calomira de Cimara and Mr Waite give " twenty-eight " ( K " Ch ") as the number of this path. The text followed by Dr Westcott gives the correct number, which is " twenty-seven."*)

The **(twenty-eighth) path** is called the **Palpable or Active Intelligence.**
HNThIB (K " Ch ") NQRA ShKL מורגש = MVRGSh.
(The simple-letter **N.** Scorpio ♏. In Tarot, **Wheel of Fortune.**)
" The (twenty-eighth) path is called the Active Intelligence, for thence is created the spirit of every creature of the supreme orb, and the activity, that is to say, the motion, to which they are subject." (Waite.)
(The path of Movement.)
(*This path is omitted by Dr Westcott. In the versions of Comtesse Calomira de Cimara and Mr Waite it is numbered the " twenty-seventh " ( K " Z "). That this is a mistake may be found by comparing the contents of this path and the twenty-seventh with the foundations of the seventh and eighth of the simple-letters ( L and N). " S. Y.," Chapter V. 13 and 14.*)

The **twenty-ninth path** is called the **Corporeal Intelligence.**
HNThIB K " T " NQRA ShKL מוגשם = MVGShMf.
(The simple-letter **S.** Sagittarius ♐. In Tarot, the **Tower.**)
" The twenty-ninth path is called the Corporeal Intelligence ; it informs every body which is incorporated under all orbs, and it is the growth thereof." (Waite.)
(The path of Wrath.)
(*In black magic this path helps the operator to come " en rapport" with his victim.*)

The **thirtieth path** is called the **Collective Intelligence.**
HNThIB " L " NQRA ShKL כללי = KLLI.

(The simple-letter **O**. Capricornus ♑. In Tarot, the **Fool**.)
" The thirtieth path is called the Collective Intelligence, for thence astrologers, by the judgment of the stars and the heavenly signs, derive their speculations and the perfection of their science according to the motions of the stars." (Waite.)
(The path of Mirth.)

The **thirty-first path** is called the **Perpetual Intelligence**.
HNThIB L " A " NQRA ShKL תמידי = ThMIDI.
(The simple-letter **Tz**. Aquarius ♒. In Tarot, the **Hermit**.)
" The thirty-first path is called the Perpetual Intelligence. Why is it so called ? Because it rules the movement of the sun and the moon according to their constitution, and causes each to gravitate in its respective orb." (Waite.)
(The path of Meditation.)
(*The ability to concentrate thought and to keep it along a given line for any length of time, even as the sun and the moon are kept in their orbs, is communicated from this path.*)

The **thirty-second path** is called the **Assisting Intelligence**.
HNThIB L " B " NQRA ShKL נעבד = NOBD.
(The simple-letter **Q**. Pisces ♓. In Tarot, **Judgment**.)
" The thirty-second path is called the Assisting Intelligence, because it directs all the operations of the seven planets, with their divisions, and concurs therein." (Waite.)
(The path of sleep.)

(*End of " The 32 Paths of Wisdom* ")

# LIST OF WORKS USED BY US IN OUR STUDY OF "SEPHER YETZIRAH"

*Text A.*—The "Mantua" edition of "Sepher Yetzirah," 1562.

*Text B.*—The text of Isaac Loria according to L. Goldschmidt, 1895.

*Text C.*—The text according to R. Saadya Gaon.

*Text D.*—The text from an Arabic Commentary on "Sepher Yetzirah" according to L. Goldschmidt, 1895.

*Cimara.*—French version of "Sepher Yetzirah," by Comtesse Calomira de Cimara, 1913 (published by Durville).

*Westcott.*—English version of "Sepher Yetzirah," by Dr W. Wynn Westcott.

*Goldschmidt.*—German version of "Sepher Yetzirah," by L. Goldschmidt, 1895.

*Postellus.*—"Abrahami Patriarchæ Liber Jezirah," by Gulielmus Postellus, 1552.

*Pistorius.*—"Artis Cabalisticæ Scriptores," a collection of Pistorius, 1587.

*Rittangelius.*—The Amsterdam Hebrew and Latin versions, by Rittangelius, 1642.

*Waite.*—"The Doctrine and Literature of the Kabalah," by A. E. Waite.